THE FEELING IS U... EVERYONE LOVES NOW...

"Reading a collection of articles by Roy Blount, Jr., is like panning for gold at Tiffany's—you know the nuggets will be there, the only question is their brilliance. Well, prepare to strike the mother lode."

Chicago Tribune

"Blount is that rare writer who can be funny and serious at the same time. . . . The reason his collection is fresh is that once he starts running he's on a course of his own."

Cleveland Plain Dealer

"Roy Blount, Jr., is a humorist to whom writing humorously comes naturally. . . . What keeps Blount's prose constantly fresh is that it's rooted in the ordinariness of human life. . . . The real distinction of Blount's talent is that he is able to strip things of their pretensions through playful ridicule."

The Pittsburgh Press

"Blount's cleverness and ability to see into the central absurdity of things are just one half of his talent as a humorist. The second half is made up of his feel and love for the language. . . . He is as sure-footed on the slippery slopes of funniness as a mountain goat on an alp."

Milwaukee Journal

"Blount's writing is firmly in that Southern tradition, its word-tumbling cadences saturated in the vernacular, but studded with allusions to classical literature that fit ironically and effectively."

Minneapolis Star Tribune

"Roy Blount, Jr., manages a delicate balancing act. He is a hard-hitting humorist who still seems down home, one of the guys. He is witty without too much self indulgence, satirical without being snide, and absolutely unbiased. Everything is on target. And Blount has a beautiful stroke. He draws readers in with a beautiful bunt, before blasting one out of the park with a swing of stinging wit."

Sacramento Union

"When Roy Blount cuts loose with his Gatling-gun humor, nothing is sacred or safe."

The Chatttanooga Times

"*Now, Where Were We?* should continue to expand America's appreciation for this talented and frequently surprising writer."

Fort Worth Star-Telegram

"Hilarious."

Houston Chronicle

Also by Roy Blount, Jr.

. . . .

ABOUT THREE BRICKS SHY OF A LOAD

CRACKERS

ONE FELL SOUP

WHAT MEN DON'T TELL WOMEN

IT GROWS ON YOU

WEBSTER'S ARK & SOUP SONGS

NOT EXACTLY WHAT I HAD IN MIND

*ABOUT THREE BRICKS SHY . . . AND THE
LOAD FILLED UP*

FIRST HUBBY

NOW, WHERE WERE WE?

Roy Blount, Jr.

NOW, WHERE WERE WE?

Ballantine Books • New York

The contents of this work were originally published in the following magazines
and newspapers: *Antaeus, Atlanta Journal-Constitution, Atlanta Weekly, The
Atlantic, Condé Nast's Traveler, Esquire, Food & Wine, Gentlemen's Quar-
terly, New York, New York Times, Penthouse, San Francisco Examiner,
Southern, Sports Illustrated, Spy,* and *TV Guide.*

Grateful acknowledgment is made to the following for permission to reprint
previously published material:

Think magazine: "If I Had Been a Delegate" by Roy Blount, Jr. Reprinted by
permission from *Think* magazine. Copyright © 1987 by International Business
Machines Corp.

USA Today: "Rita Mae Brown's Battle Hymn of the Ridiculous" by Roy
Blount, Jr. Copyright © 1986 by *USA Today.* Reprinted with permission.

Library of Congress Catalog Card Number: 90-93064

ISBN: 0-345-37032-5

This edition published by arangement with Villard Books, a division of
Random House, Inc.

Cover design by Barbara Leff
Cover photograph © Slick Lawson

Manufactured in the United States of America

First Ballantine Books Edition: October 1990

10 9 8 7 6 5 4 3 2 1

"I am a parcel of vain strivings tied by a chance bond together," wrote Thoreau, and that was *Thoreau*, right? As for this book, can one and the same person be conceived as having written all this stuff? Can any one person be expected to read it?
To us.

And to Audrey, who, like her cousins, has gumption.

Contents

· · · · · · · · · · · · · · · · · · · ·

Contents

NOW, WHERE WERE WE?

WHY IT LOOKS LIKE I WILL BE THE NEXT PRESIDENT OF THE UNITED STATES, I RECKON

(Acceptance Speech That Would Have Been Made to the Democratic Nominating Convention in Atlanta if Things Had Worked Out Right)

Well, when they said "brokered" and "somebody waiting in the wings," I never dreamed it would come around to where they meant me. And neither did they, I bet. For one thing, I figured I was part of "they." One of the ones sitting back looking down our noses at the candidates. I never thought for one minute, until recently, that I would be the one standing here looking down on everybody—but humbly, but with pride.

True, I am a Democrat, in a high-minded kind of way, and then too I grew up right outside of Atlanta here. So I know a little something about Southern politics, and I could see what the editors of *The New Republic* were getting at when they wrote in their March 7 issue, "There is something special about the South. And it's not only that Democrats can't win without winning the South. . . . Who better than a reflective and articulate Southerner can speak about Union to and for a cynical and psychologically dismantled nation?"

But still. I mean, as of March 7 I hadn't popped up *at all*, in *any* of the polls.

But then Mike Dukakis let it slip that he couldn't really regard anybody as a true Democrat who wasn't Greek, and Richard Gephardt got carried away in a speech to the League of Women Voters and declared that he had always been a woman, and Paul Simon mysteriously took to wearing an ascot, and Tipper

Gore—feeling defensive about charges that she had alienated the sixties generation—wrote a campaign song entitled "Who Says He's Got to Stop Being Beaten by His Wife?" that had suggestive lyrics in it and then ran off with Twisted Sister, and Jesse Jackson was linked with Kurt Waldheim and Bruce Babbitt turned out to be a Canadian national, and Gary Hart was photographed in bunny-foot pajamas with Jessica Hahn in Playboy and Joe Biden, while telling a labor group about his own difficulties as a worker, confessed that he owed his soul to the company store, and Mario Cuomo came out with a book of meditations entitled *I'd Rather Be Bright Than President,* and Bill Bradley had a midlife crisis and decided to forgo politics to try a comeback in the NBA, and Sam Nunn was revealed to have a brother in the warhead business who said he'd been raised to believe that capitalism meant being open-minded about who you do business with, and Ted Kennedy was endorsed by Richard Nixon, and Lee Iacocca was caught personally selling a used Chrysler with a Hyundai transmission in it at $1,200 over book value to a nun, and a stiff wind tumped the top three stories of Trump Tower over onto Fifth Avenue, and it came out that aides to Daniel Inouye had forcibly restrained him from slipping several million dollars for a Zoroastrian day-care center in Belgium into the budget bill (he confessed he couldn't stop himself, he had a craving to make weirdly inappropriate appropriations), and Warren Beatty completely lost his cool when asked about his Hart problem, and Bruce Springsteen said he wasn't really interested, and am I leaving anybody out?

Oh, and Oprah Winfrey and Phil Donahue had an actual knockdown, drag-out fight on *McNeil-Lehrer,* and a computer was disclosed in Ted Koppel's hair, and Pat Schroeder got the giggles, and William Hurt cried, and Molly Ringwald turned out not to be old enough, and Henry Cisneros and several other up-and-coming young hopefuls said they wanted to wait until after the Depression started, and Gregory Peck said he wouldn't run unless he could dress up like Lincoln, and Ed Asner came over as too grumpy, and Kissin' Jim Folsom turned out to be dead, and both Michael Jackson and Walter Cronkite said they weren't really interested. And Ed Koch was overheard remarking that he didn't like American food. And Mikhail Gorbachev said he wasn't really interested but Raisa might be if the deal was right, which seemed a bit much.

Oh, and Walter Mondale said he was kind of tired, but he might like to be vice-president again. And Jimmy Carter got his feelings hurt because it took so long before he figured in the speculation. And several other Kennedys were endorsed by Richard Nixon.

Well, even then I held back. I didn't want to be seen as thrusting myself forward, and my chief adviser—W. E. "Slick" Lawson of Nashville, author of the country song title "I Won the Dance Contest Last Night but I Can't Take the Trophy Home"—agreed that that was wise, partly because he wanted to thrust himself forward.

So did several other of my articulate and reflective Southern friends. But while they were drinking and hollering, "You 'bout as reflective and articulate as a sick dominecker chicken's breakfast" at one another, I was testing the waters.

I made a speech to the American Association of Businessmen Just About Barely Breaking Even What with the Way Things Are Going convention at Vail, Colorado. In that address I put forward some of my commonsense economic proposals:

• Reduce the federal deficit by citizen participation that is *bound,* if things add up at all, to pump money into the Treasury without the government having to do anything hardly at all: Everybody go down to the post office and buy two rolls of stamps and throw them away.

• Restore Wall Street to a sound foundation by requiring every securities transaction to be cash on the barrelhead, no bill larger than a twenty.

• Make the dollar less silly by knocking the last digit off of every sum of money in America. Thus ballplayers would make

$100,000, the national debt would be down in the low hundred billions, and a cup of coffee would be a nickel.

• Restore the draft, not for young men but for corporate executives making over $1 million a year including bonuses and weasel deals.

• Explore the cost-effectiveness of putting able-bodied homeless persons through Outward Bound. (This was Slick's idea, and caused controversy, enabling me to show my toughness by firing him. I had already gotten out of him what I wanted, a campaign-song title: "I Will Treat You Like Your Momma Used to—Then Let's See 'Em Send Me Off to Jail.")

See, one thing a Southern articulate and reflective person feels it incumbent upon him to do is to be simple. You got to put the kibble over where the slow dogs can get some. I shouldn't be the one to say it, but these proposals gave me a populist appeal.

Still I perceived that I was being perceived as too abstract and austere. A writer, not a politician. I knew enough about the Southern political tradition to realize that Ronald Reagan had mastered three important aspects of it *aside* from simple proposals:

1. Lying.
2. Easing folks' minds.
3. Setting an example of the feasibility of getting away with things.

I went to an image consultant. Told her I was just trying to gather material for my writing, and asked her what if I had a friend who looked and sounded exactly like me but was too shy to come in himself. She prescribed a slight hitch in this friend's gitalong, which makes me less threatening and accentuates my homespunness, and also sold me an exact copy of the suit that Jimmy Stewart wore in *Mr. Smith Goes to Washington*, only colorized.

And before I knew it I was carrying myself more presidentially. A big media consultant came up to me on the street—didn't even know who I was—and said he had worked out a way through modern editing techniques to produce a TV spot of Will Rogers endorsing me.

"Won't the newspapers raise some questions about that?" I asked.

He said he had already fixed up a clip of Will Rogers saying, "All I know is what I see on the television."

But I didn't want to rely on electronic gimmickry. And I didn't want to focus on myself too much. That way I wouldn't have to be denying things all the time. The Reagan administration lost the people's trust because word got out that the Iran-Contra thing was based on "plausible deniability." Here is how plausible deniability works:

When an administration is accused of something, its spokesman says, "Nothing could be further from the truth." In other words, "We don't see any way you can prove it, at least not for a while yet."

Then when evidence supporting the accusation comes out, the spokesman can say, "Well, some things could be further from the truth, but this is not at all the kind of thing we would do."

Further evidence comes out. "Quite a few things could be further from the truth, maybe, but we could prove this isn't exactly the truth, if it weren't for national security reasons."

Irrefutable evidence comes out. "Well, let's say it is the truth. But we didn't know it was the truth."

Then, "At any rate the president himself didn't know anything about it."

Then, finally, "There are no documents showing that the president ever told his wife. And we cannot comment on any further details because they are all subjects of litigation."

Somehow or another, in regard to the Iran-Contra thing, this didn't go over. Maybe the Reagan administration should have taken a page from Jim Folsom, who took the position "I always plead guilty." What a Southern politician might have said, right from the beginning, was "We done it and it seemed like a good idea at the time but them damn Iranians lied. Them damn Iranians can't be trusted any further than you can throw 'em and I'd like to hear 'em deny it. But the deal looked like it would be good for a lot of loyal Americans and friends of America and if you can't be loyal to your loyal American friends then what good are you?" I don't know whether that would have worked, but it couldn't have worked much worse than what the Reagan administration tried.

Still, the more I thought about this plausible deniability thing, the more I felt instinctively that the American people would go for it—the American people *like* plausibility—if somehow they could all be let in on it. So here's what I proposed, in a speech to the American Leeway Council. I proposed that the right to plausible deniability be extended to every American citizen.

Phone company calls you, says, "You haven't paid your bill in two months and you owe us two hundred and nineteen dollars."

You say, "Nothing could be further from the truth."

That confuses the phone company a little. "What do you mean by that?"

You say, "Well, I think my words speak for themselves."

Phone company: "Listen—all right, you have a telephone, right?"

"First I've heard of it," you say. "News to me."

The phone company gets exercised: *"What do you mean, you don't know you have a telephone? We're talking to you on your telephone!"*

That's where you have to hang tough. You say, "That's your opinion."

And there are several different telephone companies out there in this great competitive land, so you've got some play.

Well, there is nothing Americans like better than some play. As one man, the American Leeway Council rose to give me a standing ovation—but I stayed them with a gesture and broke into the Plausible Deniability Song:

> *Say you been cheating on your diet,*
> *Or you went out and started a riot,*
> *All you have to do is just . . . deny it.*
>   *Deee-niability,*
>   *You don't have to have no humility,*
>   *If you've got de-ni-a-bil-i-ty.*
>   *And remember: you . . . didn't hear it from me.*

Well, "went over" is putting it mildly. If there's anybody who feels the burden of our being a debtor nation, it is the American Leeway Council. They whooped. They hollered. They carried me down to the marina proper and gave me a sixty-foot boat.

This was the crucial moment. The temptation was to rest on my laurels. But I saw that I was verging now on not being austere enough. So when interviewers came to me and asked about the bottom line, I said it was about time we opened the presidency to competitive bidding. And I came out with my ace-in-the-hole slogan:

"Just Pay Me What Ike Made."

Whooo, did interviewers' eyes light up. Even the ones who didn't want me to get away with it saw that I was golden.

"I believe I can get along," I said, "what with two nice free houses city and country *and* free haircuts, on Ike's seventy-five thousand."

Saves the nation $125,000 a year right there. And reminds us of the fifties, which are coming back (if we keep our fingers crossed that it isn't the thirties), and of course when you're invoking Ike you're invoking bipartisan appeal. And you're offering balm to a long-festering old Southern resentment: over the fact that because of the Democratic Party, so many Southerners, or anyway their parents, found themselves voting for Adlai Stevenson.

And the next thing I knew the phone rang and it was old Bob Strauss saying, "I bleeve, Scooter, it is time for you and me to sit down with a few of the boys."

And here I am. I thank you for the nomination. And if I have come this far this fast over every other Democrat in America, I don't see why I can't whip one measly wore-out Republican.

(Prolonged demonstration on the floor.)

And I pledge this to you:

When I am elected I will honor the office by staying in it. Out of America's way. Ronald Reagan has already demonstrated that the president who seems to get the most things done is the president who lets things go.

He was good at that because he was an actor. I'll be good at it because I'm a writer. Four years at $75,000 per is a heck of a book advance. I'll bet three-fourths of Southern literature was produced for less than $300,000, all together. I'm going to *write* my presidency. And you won't have to worry about how I'm doing till the book comes out, in the fall of 1992.

Then I will go on my promotion tour—also my reelection campaign. And the talk hosts will flip through my five-hundred-odd pages of solid accomplishment and ask me, "Are you sure you didn't just make this up?"

And I will say, "Nothing could be further from the truth."

I.
LOST AND FOUND

0 *LOST!*

. . .

I write this in Maharaja Class on Air India, chewing betel nuts and feeling good and lost.

I was not brought up to chew betel nuts, which is one reason I took them, instead of mints, when the flight attendant came by with a tray of assorted little things to put in your mouth. Betel nuts, I understand, are mildly narcotic, but as far as I can tell they are just vaguely pungent to crunch.

"I see that you have taken the betel nuts," the Bombay businessman next to me remarked a few minutes ago, by way of an icebreaker. "Tell me, in America is confidence placed in *Time* magazine?"

As I mulled my response, a barefoot man in a filmy orange robe came down the aisle, looking wobbly, and entered the lavatory. A man in Western clothes followed as far as the door and stood guard. On his shirt he wore a name tag that said YOGI SECURITY.

All this spectacle, and I am just returning from London to New York by the cheapest available means. (Luck got me into Maharaja Class—Tourist was overbooked.) Last time I made this trip I had an even better fare on Kuwait Airways, only we arrived at JFK twenty-four hours late. Weather forced us to land in Gander, Newfoundland, and take a bus to Grand Falls, where I spent the night in a motel room with a Kuwaiti gentleman.

"Hello," I said to him. "My name's Roy Blount and I never expected to wind up tonight in Grand Falls, Newfoundland."

"Please?" he said.

"Hello," I said to him. "My name's Roy Blount and I never expected to wind up tonight in Grand Falls, Newfoundland."

"I don't know," he said.

Now here I am exchanging views with an Indian. "You have a singer," he says. "She is called Madonna?"

Maybe the betel nuts are kicking in, but I think what I am feeling is just an effect of travel: the kind of disorientation that seems *right* somehow. Outside is all clouds. Maybe we'll put down tonight in Beulah land. Meanwhile I am lost.

I'm going to say about being lost what I once heard a seemingly tasteful sex therapist say (I wasn't consulting her, this was at a wedding) about the vaginal orgasm: It's right up my alley. I was born lost, and do not consider it a problem.

To say that, of course, is to stray somewhat—I don't know how far, is the trouble—from the truth. Being lost is in a sense *the* problem of life. Being lost and in dire need of a lavatory is terrible. Being lost with someone else is a real—therefore most often a regrettable—test of a relationship. Families, for instance, should think it over very carefully before getting lost together. The best people to get lost with are those who are very loose about it. My friend Slick Lawson and some friends of his were in the chase car following a hot-air balloon when they found themselves on a dirt road somewhere in Tennessee that did not show up on their map. "We're lost," one of them said. But the country morning air was easy to take, *they* weren't the ones who had just disappeared over the tree line in a balloon, and they enjoyed one another's company. "How can we be lost," said the driver, "when we don't care where we are?"

Not long ago I was lost, briefly, in the Peruvian rain forest with three people whom I had known for just a few hours. There we were, surrounded by vegetation that did not ring a bell. The trail had trailed out. When we retraced our steps, they trailed out too. Questions of leadership threatened to arise. I hate it when questions of leadership arise. In travel, as in life, I like the idea that there must be some mutually rewarding—even if not readily comprehensible—middle ground where leadership isn't required. But if one person wants to go in a direction that he has a hunch is east, and another wants to go in a different direction that *he* feels is east, and a third wants to go in still another direction that she believes to be west (but which is not the opposite of either of the other directions), and no one can tell where the sun is exactly, and no one can remember which side of a tree moss grows on *or* whether it's the same below the equator, then where's your middle ground? In a way I wanted to sit there by myself, in the rain forest, and appreciate being lost. On the other hand, it was a relief to hear an American voice not far away calling out, "Wait up, something sucked off my shoe," and another one replying, *"Something?"* Other travelers, it turned out, were on the path.

The path. There's something too single-minded about that notion. The rut. Yet we could not live without linearity.

Betel nuts are about as near to a controlled substance as I get into these days, but back during the Nixon administration I liked trying to think on strong marijuana. With other people, even. We'd sit there seeing what kind of sense we could make. I still have a tape recording of one such session:

"Wait a minute," a friend's voice says. "This is not the train of thought."

"If this is not the train of thought," says another friend's voice, "then what is it the train of?" I remember that this seemed an extraordinarily thought-provoking question at the time.

I am off on a tangent here. I set out to recount anecdotes of being lost around the world. (My friend Christabel King once drove up to the Aswan Dam and asked two Egyptian men the way to Khartoum. One of them pointed to the left. The other pointed across the first one's arm to the right. The first one said, "*Tawali*," which is Arabic for "forward." Then they resumed their conversation.)

But here's what interests me at the moment: why being lost makes me feel as though I've gotten back home. When I was growing up in Georgia in the Methodist Church, we sang "I once was lost, but now am found," but it wasn't that simple. Most of the hymns were about getting somewhere better:

> *. . . a higher plane than I have found,*
> *Lord plant my feet on higher ground.*

To me there was something rambunctious about those songs of uplift. They may have made other congregants feel more rooted, but they made my mind rise and wander.

"When did you decide to leave the South?" I once asked Joe Frazier, the great heavyweight fighter, whose boyhood was spent in South Carolina.

"As soon as I heard there was a North," he said. "I took the first train smoking." But Lord knows the North is not the answer. When I talked to Frazier, he was back in South Carolina buying a farm. I think whatever part of the world I might have grown up in would have made me want to be transported.

The first time I was ever seriously lost I must have been about seven. My parents took me along on a Sunday drive to visit friends in what were then the exurbs of Atlanta. Since adult conversation made me want to scream, I went out back of the house to play in the woods. I loved woods because they were all dirt and disorder. I felt engrossed and pagan in them. But when I figured it was time to return to civilization, I came out on an asphalt road. I walked off up it, and persisted for what seemed like hours, thinking, "I don't see how it can be this far, but . . ." I was going somewhere by myself.

There weren't many houses out that way, but finally I stopped and rang a doorbell. An adult opened the door. I asked if he knew where the Boozers lived. He said no and shut the door.

I'd never met a grown-up who wouldn't help a seven-year-old kid before. I felt *justified,* in a way. A citizen of the world. Adult homeowners *weren't* always models of conduct. Any more than I was. This was interesting. This was travel.

But I was road-weary. Another house came along, I turned myself in again, and this time the people looked the Boozers up in the phone book and called. No one answered.

I wasn't worried. If I had not been secure in the knowledge that my parents would never take the opportunity of my disappearance to run off somewhere with the Boozers, I would have been a different kind of traveler. (Neither my parents nor the Boozers, I might mention, drank.) "They're probably all out looking for you," the good samaritans assured me, and that made sense; but it also brought me down a bit, made me feel less footloose.

These nice folks drove me to the Boozers', where my parents were just coming up out of the woods. My mother was in a state. "I could just *see* you out there, facedown in the creek," she said. I was glad to get back to her, just as I am always glad to see America again, but I never quite accepted the fairness of her being *mad* at me, until I became a parent and from time to time it hit me that one of my kids was out of pocket, maybe gone forever, maybe even *looking* to get lost without realizing the risks that wanderers run.

The risks that keep fresh the strangeness of being anywhere. As I was writing the above, two more yogis were accompanied to the lavatory. "They are going to a convention," I was informed by the man next to me. "They were not true samadhi. They have not renounced the world." The world! I should think not.

In the Nashville airport recently my sister Susan saw a couple of Indian newlyweds, fresh from the ceremony, trying to get through security. They were bedizened in gold-encrusted clothes and golden rings of every description, so you can imagine how they set off the metal detector. They were taking rings off their fingers, rings off their ears, maybe bells off their toes, certainly rings out of their noses, when a kindly security woman stopped them. "Now honey, you just never going to get through," she told the bride. "We just going to run the wand over you."

I FIND MYSELF
AT A SPA?

I have sold out to health. I who love chili dogs more—a great deal more—than (just in and of itself) fresh air. I have started going around saying things like "No one should eat olives. They're full of sodium!" I love olives! I have made my way through inches of sheer gin to reach olives. I never switched over to a twist, either, when olives in one's drink became unfashionable. You can't eat a twist! Or if you do eat a twist, it is for the sake of the vitamins, and I have always held that it is morally wrong to eat with an ulterior motive.

I love gin, for that matter.

And fried things. To me, good fried chicken, or good fried anything else—fried *calamari,* which I never had till I was thirty-two—is like an old and close friend. For me, to come upon something that is fried well and not eat it is like running into someone who helped raise me and cutting him dead. I am a part of all that I have et, and I have polished off with relish—in every sense of that word—everything from Stroganoff to buffalo.

But now I have sold out to health. I who live by such philosophers as Abe Lemons, the college basketball coach, who once explained that he didn't jog because "When I die, I want to be *sick*"; and Will Campbell, the preacher, who decided not to quit chewing tobacco because "I didn't want to be a slave to my own willpower." I who have never been able to take herbs seriously, because they always make me think of someone named Herb. (Not anyone in particular, although herb tea makes me think of Mr. T if his first name were Herb.)

I went through the Executive Renewal Program (I who secretly feel that all executives should be canceled!) at the Canyon Ranch Spa in Tucson, Arizona, and—like an American pilot who is shot down in North Korea and stays on to become minister of defense—I sold out to health.

You notice I say *health*. Not *wellness*. Give me that much credit. *Wellness* is the term they use at Canyon Ranch. That is the only thing that struck me as unhealthy about Canyon Ranch. *Holistic*—another term that I would like to keep an eye on for ten or fifteen years before I start using it—is what comes naturally to some of the Canyon Ranch staff, but management feels that *wellness* appeals more to people who can afford to attend a spa.

I can't afford to attend a spa. I went to Canyon Ranch with an idea that it would be chockablock with pampered plutocratic porkers who would be standing around in the locker room saying, as W. C. Fields said in *My Little Chickadee,* only they would be saying it with less resonance, "I believe I will dip my pink-and-white body in yon Roman tub. I feel a bit gritty after the affairs of the day." Canyon Ranch, of course, hopes that corporations will send their harried, overweight, unwell executives through the roughly $2,000 program, and that after seven days of exercise, proper diet, massage, and tips on stress reduction they will return renewed, refreshed, reborn, and ready to earn still greater profits. Not me. I planned to have a good time, in more ways than one, at Canyon Ranch's expense.

I never thought I would become a new person. (If I had, I would have been shopping around, trying to find the right one.)

I figured I would lose a few pounds, clear away a little cranial fog, squeeze a little sludge out of my system. I never dreamed I would get carried away.

Of course, when I go out on a story, I tend to *go with,* as the saying goes, whatever is going on. If I were doing a story about rabbit torturing, I wouldn't go with that, of course, but—for instance, the last time I had been in Tucson before my week at Canyon Ranch was with Jerry Jeff Walker, the singer. I was writing a story eventually entitled "I May Have Sung with Jerry Jeff." I stayed up for forty-eight hours having a hell of a time in five or six of the ten ways you can kill yourself having a hell of a time, and wound up on the stage of the Tucson Community Center Music Hall singing—or so I was told the next day, and did in part remember—"Pissing in the Wind" with Jerry Jeff and his band. I figure that story took five years off my life, and now, thanks to Canyon Ranch, Tucson and I are even.

With the Canyon Ranch story, however, I went further than usual. For the last few years I have been feeling—at those moments when I couldn't help noticing how I felt—like a pile of old leaves. And Executive Renewal made me feel like a young jackrabbit.

Full of bounce and lusting after carrots. As I write this, it has been five weeks since I slouched off toward Tuscon—*and I am still Renewed.* Thank God Canyon Ranch isn't run by the Reverend Moon; I'd be in some airport right now asking people for money. *I continue to get more and more Renewed.*

In one week at Canyon Ranch I lost eight pounds, and in the four weeks since returning home—although those weeks included Christmas and New Year's (the season of Baked Goods and Punch)—I have lost eight more pounds and started looking more nearly like Sly Stallone than, frankly, I want to.

You ought to see me! It's incredible! I look eight years younger! You ought to listen to me talk about it! I would bore your ass off! Speaking of which, I have—for me—hardly any ass left. I who can't stand people who have hardly any ass!

I would rather have Fatty Arbuckle's body than Sly Stallone's! I would rather have Fatty Arbuckle's *career*! I have never known anybody whose body was perfect-looking who was worth a shit. My body is not all that great-looking, even yet, except in a certain light, but for the first time I find it, frankly, attractive. I don't mean that it attracts *me,* but still I don't think this is sexually healthy. It wouldn't surprise me now to find out I can dance.

It is only now, as I write this, that I realize how deep into health I have slipped. Do you know what I am doing, literally, as I write this? I mean, in between paragraphs? I am eating plain yogurt mixed with wheat germ and granola! As a matter of fact, since I learned in Executive Renewal that granola is too honeyed to be ideally healthy, I am eating plain yogurt, wheat germ and granola *with a sense of sin*!

And do you know what I am going to do when I finish this scratchy, sour breakfast that I have come to enjoy? I am going to go lift my son's weights. I who only months ago was trying to get up the energy to write a piece comparing weight lifting to the arms race!

And after I lift weights, I am going to ride my daughter's stationary bicycle ten miles. As I ride I may write a song. But it won't be a sad love song such as I used to write, like "I Found One of Your Old Bobby Pins This Morning in My Heart." I'm not partial to heartbreak anymore. I'm a lean, mean writing machine. If I write a song on that nonrolling wheel, it will have more beat and uplift than meaning; it will be called something like "Doin' What Aorta."

Let me try to explain what happened to me at Canyon Ranch. The week before I went there I took care to eat a lot of French toast and get up to 196 pounds, which is about the top of my range, though I have been higher. Even before Executive Renewal I knew 196 pounds was stretching things a bit, and I knew I ought to be eating and drinking less than I was and exercising more than I was, which was not at all except every once in a while when I would exercise too much.

But I had always held to traditional feelings about exercise: that people aren't meant to run unless they have something to run from or after, and that the only honest reason to be heavily muscled is so people will know you are a blacksmith. About food: that you ought to eat as much as you can whenever you can, because you never know. And about drink: that it makes you sing better.

And when it came to weighing 196, my reasoning was this: After all, I didn't smoke, I was six foot one, I couldn't think of a single great writer who wasn't built funny, I had not lost my quickness at pulling in my stomach when I passed a mirror, and I could still go hard after a pork chop or a tennis ball when push came to shove. So how rotten a shape could I be in? Even if I did feel like an owl had died in my chest. Hey, I was forty-two.

Then at Canyon Ranch they took calipers to me and measured my percentage of body fat. I had always dreaded three scientific reckonings: (1) Just Exactly What He Knows About Whatever He Is Talking About, (2) How Much He Has Ever Done for Other People in Proportion to How Hard He Has Tried to Get Out of It and (3) What Portion of Him Is Congealed Grease. Now I knew the answer to (3). My blood ran cold.

When they test your pecentage of body fat, they find out how much of your body weight is blood, hair, skin, eyeballs, bone, muscle, spit, fillings, *Weltschmerz,* sleepydust, viscera, your last meal, and miscellaneous, on the one hand, and how much is fat, on the other. My body, it turned out, was 84 percent fat.

Actually, the figure was somewhat less high. I exaggerate. I do not intend to publish what my percentage of body fat was. Let's say it was high. Let's say I had enough fat on me to manufacture an entire, if shapeless, ten-year-old child. And a box of candles.

Executive Renewal included a complete physical, something I had not undergone since the army. This examination revealed that I had the heart and lungs of a three-year-old horse and the stomach of a working camel, but everything else was at best human. My cholesterol was above average, and according to the calipers I was carrying enough extra weight to handicap Whirl-away, in his prime, head-to-head against Edwin Meese in a full business suit.

What if Edwin Meese were to challenge me someday? Call me up out of the blue and say, "You don't think much of our admin-istration, huh? I'll race you over eight furlongs and you can ride a horse. Any horse you can climb up on. I'll just go in my wing tips. How about it?"

But I could have rationalized my way out of worrying about that. Probably Meese wouldn't call, and if he did, I could always say that I couldn't find a horse willing to line up alongside him.

What turned me into this abject tool of the health interests was not body-fat shame, or even heart-attack fear. True, my grandfather died of a heart attack at seventy while working in the yard, and my father of a heart attack at sixty right after working in the yard, but I figured I could evade that trap by staying out of the yard. I didn't welcome death, but then I didn't welcome alfalfa sprouts either. (My feeling about alfalfa sprouts was, if they are so good for you, why do they look like hair?) Anyway, hey, I did great on that treadmill thing with all the electrodes stuck to me. You can't listen to as much country music as I do without developing your heart.

The crucial subversive thing that happened to me at Canyon Ranch was that I learned to stop rationalizing (which is just my life's work, that's all—out the window) and love wellness. Health! Health! Did I say wellness? Oh, my soul.

There we were up on a mountain, surrounded by cactus, more mountains, and miles and miles of air with no additives in it. There were seven of us in this session of Executive Renewal. (The ranch as a whole takes up to 140 guests at a time—always enough people around for a variety of brisk goings-on, but never much of a crowd.) All of us except writer Blair Sabol, an admitted fitness obsessive, and Larry Saliterman, a holistic dentist-entrepreneur from Minneapolis, were out of shape. And Saliterman, who now looks like Roy Scheider, *used* to be thirty pounds overweight and walk like a duck ("I looked *stupid,*" he says) before he got into wellness. Health.

For a week we ingested no refined sugar, caffeine, or liquor, and scarcely any salt or fats. The men ate 1,000 calories a day, the women 800. But the food was very good, and we could arrange the various options on the menu any way we chose within our calorie limits. And we could go over the limit if we wanted to.

We could do anything we wanted to. Hey, I'm an American. I don't like places where I can't do anything I want to. On the other hand, one afternoon a member of the grounds crew was fooling around with a tangerine tree when I passed, and he suggested I pick myself a couple. I was eating the second one as I joined the group. "Right off the tree," I said happily to a member of the wellness staff.

Who did not look overjoyed for me. It had never crossed my mind, in my life, that there could be any transgression involved in eating two tangerines. "Guy on the grounds crew . . . ," I said. "Nice guy . . . Suggested I . . ." The member of the wellness staff did not come right out and ask me whether this grounds crew guy was sort of sinuous-looking and had scales, but there was a hint of that question in her eyes. I had eaten something that, although nutritious, was an off-the-menu bunch of calories.

And I was not offended by this consideration. I was not alienated from the tangerine tree—in fact, I frequented it throughout the rest of the week—but I had learned what Eve learned: There is no such thing as a free snack.

Now, whenever I take a bite of anything, I am conscious not only of how it tastes and of what a wonderful experience bite taking is in general, but also of what that bite is doing for me and what it is costing me healthwise. It actually makes eating more interesting. It makes carrots taste better, and rum cake (which Canyon Ranch does not serve) more death-defying.

If health should make food lose its savor, then forget health.

But we had a good time at the Canyon Ranch table. One of our group, Suzanne de Passe, a movie executive with Motown, was a genius at such improvisations as mock sour cream made of Gulden's mustard (which has hardly any calories) and mozzarella curds (cottage cheese has too much fat). We had very little red meat, but we did have a steak one night that was the size of my thumb and that I found ingratiating.

One group met with John Lopis, who was head of Executive Renewal, in daily Focus Sessions. These gave us a chance to sound off. Stan Fink, a North Dakota haberdasher of great Dakotan renown, gusto, musicality, and bulk, spoke with great power of his need to overeat. He said he had been known to sneak out of bed in the middle of the night and eat, frozen, a loaf of bread hidden by his wife in the freezer. Jerry Nachman, an acerbic NBC news executive, made a heroic case all week for the benefits of smoking, staying in a chair, and eating several-pound lobsters at the Palm. Ralph Caputo of NFL Films, just by dint of his calm substantiality and an occasional fond allusion, eloquently evoked his wife's Italian cooking. I myself kept issuing such pronouncements as "I would rather die *right now* than stop enjoying my food."

These arguments we made did not hold up, however, in the face of how good we were beginning to feel. It struck me even as I was issuing the above-mentioned pronouncement, for instance, that it was very like a country song title I wrote some years ago—"I'd Give My Right Arm (to Hold You in My Arms Again)."

The proof that health had something going for it was in the pudding. The pudding was a combination of Mediterranean Melon Balls, biking in the mountains, pelvic tilts, breathing tips, trampoline time, Vegetable Medley With Sherried Truffle Sauce, herbal wraps, swimming, lipid advisories, Crab in Papaya Cup, stretching, brisk walks, and deep massage.

I didn't feel starved. I didn't feel tired. I didn't feel bored. On the first day I did think I was going to go crazy if I had to sit around any longer listening to people talk about their bodies as if they were endlessly fascinating motorcycles, and on the second day I had a headache, and the first thing I did after leaving Canyon Ranch was drink the finest-tasting airport beer and eat the most succulent airport hot dog I have ever put to my lips, but I am able to report to you in tones of astonishment that a rigorously healthy regimen agreed with me. And that I still eschew coffee, butter, and ice cream, use Gulden's mustard instead of salt wherever possible, eat as many raw vegetables and fruits as I can, take smaller meals and fewer drinks, and break a serious sweat nearly every day. So sue me. At the end of the week they tested our cholesterol and fat-in-the-blood levels again, and mine were way down.

There are more sybaritic spas than Canyon Ranch, and there are spas that are more like Marine camp. There are also places where you find wellness by eating whole, unprocessed groat kernels while meditating in the inverted frog position. At Canyon Ranch you talk to guys in the steam room who say their wives dragged them to snootier spas that made them want to throw up. The exercise at Canyon Ranch is as strenuous as you want it to be. The Canyon Ranch fitness director is named Karma, but her last name is Kientzler and she didn't get her first name in the waters of the Ganges or in Marin County. She was going to be Jackie Lynn but her father thought that wasn't "sophisticated enough for my little girl," so he named her Karma Lynn. Her sisters are named Colleen and Mignon. Karma taught me to stand up straight. I liked it.

The hiking director at Canyon Ranch, Phyllis Hochman, is a wonderful person who has walked her way out of crippling arthritis and has a great hiking dog.

I could go on and on. Because I have all this energy now.

That old health magic got me in its spell. That's the important thing. You don't want to hear about my haircut now. You want to know where I stand on poultry skin.

Wellness takes the position that poultry skin has too much fat in it. So you should peel the epidermal succulence off your turkey or your chicken or your duck before you eat it.

Here is my position: Poultry skin—crispy, bronze, juicy, imbued with every basting known to man—is a major food group. The healthier you are, the more poultry skin you can afford to eat.

I *JUST WANT WHAT*
LIZ ALWAYS HAS

. . . .

I read in one of the gossip columns that New York's Hôtel Plaza Athénée was fondly bracing itself for the arrival of Elizabeth Taylor because—*partly* because—she was known there as a person who ran up room-service bills of $2,500 a day.

How? *Condé Nast's Traveler* felt that it was in the public interest to find out what this impossible sum could buy. What would it be like to have unlimited room service?

Although I know Taylor (I call her that, not having a sexist bone in my body) only through her work, I am linked with another raven-haired, strong-willed Englishwoman, Christabel— who, although she votes Labour, consented to join me in excess. We checked into the Plaza Athénée, with no luggage.

That was going to be the first occasion for me to holler, "Oh! Right! Just because Elizabeth Taylor probably arrives with thirty-nine items of Vuitton, an Ultrasuede-sweatered saluki, and coachmen four, I guess that means that our twenty-five hundred dollars a day is not as good as hers! Is that what you're telling us, you Franklin Pangborn–looking sumbitch with your monocle and your minimal mustache and your froggified ways?"

But it was no such occasion. The receptive, if less than hail-fellow, waistcoated man at the eighteenth-century ormolu reception desk in the marble-floored lobby on two levels divided by a faux-stone balustrade did not turn a hair. He let us register!

Don't ask me why. Sure, we probably looked distinguished in an *intrinsic* regard, but it must have been plain as day that we were writing-class people out for a dubious lark in patently mass-produced shoes. If I'd been such a hotel's first line of defense I would at least have asked us to step back outside until we could get richer and more serious expressions on our faces, to go with the looks on all the other guests in the lobby, whom I took to be marquises. (Christabel, who has traveled widely, said no, they were simply hotel gentry, who are born and bred in large suites and never know life *without* room service.)

But this character didn't even exclaim, *"Bon Dieu! A green* Amex card! It is to laugh!" He must have thought Christabel was a marchioness. He let us sign the register. We went up to the room.

Accompanied by someone whom I supposed was a bellman. Imagine my chagrin when I read in the in-room literature that all guests of the Plaza Athénée are escorted to their rooms by members of management. Still, he looked like a bellman to me, except that he wasn't carrying anything. He took $10, I know that, and was quite decent about it. I had never tipped a bellman *or* a member of management $10 before in my life, but I figured I ought to get the word moving that we were there to spend.

If he was management, you'd think he would have curled his lip at the tip on the grounds that it was not enough or too much or both. "Shall I . . . put this in the safe for you?" or "Sorry, we are not in need of fresh capital at this time" is what I'd have said if I'd been managment, but that's probably why I'm not management. Too much pride. Probably members of management all over the world would be perfectly gracious about it if you gave them $10, from Leona Helmsley right on down.

In fact that's probably how they save up to pay for their own room-service bills on the road. Good Lord Almighty! A half hour after check-in, we'd already spent $330.66 (and were still hungry). Not counting the ten bucks to management and $315 for the room itself, which had nice wallpaper and a bathroom of

Portuguese rose Aurora marble but frankly was not large. Pinched a bit at the sides.

I probably should have sent the room back, but I was already worried about being indicted for bribing management, and I had been cautioned by *Condé Nast's Traveler* to stay in a room of mid-range price. If I'd gone for one of the $2,100-a-day suites, we wouldn't have been squeezing past carts and manicurists. We would have had more room-service capacity.

Fortunately, my agent, Esther, is not—in the narrow, physical, sense—large. We had her in for Taittinger champagne (one bottle, $140), beluga caviar (one dab, $95), and Florida shrimp ($13.50 for a half dozen), which did not take up much room either. The Florida shrimp were in fact less robust than the ones I had caught two weeks before with my friend Vereen at Alligator Point, Florida, by dragging a net through the surf as low and as fast as we could—you could see those scooters leaping, six inches long and bigger around than your thumb. That was some eating.

The shrimp we caught at Alligator Point, I mean. The room-service shrimp weren't bad, but I bet you get bigger ones in the suites. The caviar was nice, too, and the Taittinger was champagne, all right! You wouldn't want to waste it by shaking it up and spraying it at your girlfriend and your agent, so I didn't.

But let me say this: I've had a lot better times in hotel rooms for less money. And not even with women, necessarily. I remember one night in Itta Bena, Mississippi, sitting in a Trave-Lodge or something until five in the morning with bourbon and boiled chitlins and soda crackers and hot sauce and coaches from predominantly black colleges. Of course the food had been brought in from outside; and then too I tasted bourbon and chitlins all through the next day, and never (in that combination) again; but I remember somebody saying that night about a strait-laced colleague, "He don't know anything, because he's never done anything *wrong*."

There was something wrong about spending $2.25 *a shrimp,*

not counting the room-service charge of $2.50 *a person* (and Esther wouldn't hide), 8.25 percent sales tax, and 17 percent gratuity. So, let's see: three people six shrimp, figure each shrimp's share of . . . The way I work it out, even with the champagne and caviar carrying the bulk of the per-person costs, that means each shrimp actually prorated out to $3.13. And like I say, they were nice, but nowhere near as gratifying as the ones at Alligator Point.

Esther went off home to read books, and our friends Greg and Madeline came over and we ordered up a lot of things for dinner. The steamed langoustines in stock with asparagus tips I don't recommend, because the langoustines were lukewarm and mushy; but the turbot dish was good, and I believe the salmon tart was well received. Dinner for four was only $341.93, because we cut back to a $60 Möet et Chandon champagne and Greg was just back from Louisiana and therefore not very hungry.

We had altogether I believe three, *maybe* four, *maybe* five, bottles of a very-nice-and-why-the-hell-not-at-$57-a-bottle chablis, and while doing so we found that we could climb out a window and crawl onto a pea-gravel-covered ledge there on the fifteenth floor and get some breeze and look out onto East Sixty-fifth Street and talk about life. Try to find a perch like that at an Econo Lodge or something. There was litter on the ledge—champagne bottles that guests had tossed down from the upper floors the way people in tenements jettison chicken bones—but that wasn't a problem.

The problem was, room service was losing its fascination. I had envisioned a situation where anything was orderable-up: fireworks, jugglers, tiara rentals. As it turned out, I couldn't even get my socks done. Just as in a Holiday Inn or something, they would have had to be turned in before ten that morning—at which time they had not been dirty and we had not been in the hotel.

Greg and Madeline left, after giving us every assurance that they had had a pretty good time. My editor, Maggie, had phoned earlier to ask whether we had ordered anything *wild*. I called down and asked for an eagle.

"Excuse me?" said an accent that I pegged as Schweitzer-deutsch.

"An American eagle. It doesn't have to be alive. We need it to settle an argument. Stuffed would do."

A lighter but stranger accent came on and said, "Sir?"

"Okay, some chigger medication," I said. "We have just come from the North Georgia mountains, where tiny, near-microscopic insects—chiggers, or redbugs if you prefer—burrow into axial areas of the body. And mine are beginning to act up."

"Sir?" And the tone was that of a person who was thoughtful, ingenuous, busy, eager to serve, perhaps Burmese, and sincerely a stranger to the whole notion of chigger bites. I felt small.

"Oh, don't mind me," I said. "How about a dozen oysters?"

"I'm sorry, sir, there are none."

A serious delinquency, no oysters at two in the morning. But probably not this voice's fault. "What can I have been thinking?" I said lightly. "Plaza Athénée has no *R*'s in it." After I said this two or three more times, the voice seemed to be coming around toward seeing the drollery involved. Then we were disconnected.

Christabel, I noticed, was asleep. It was up to me. Twenty-four-hour, top-of-the-line room service was my oyster, but it lacked oysters. There must be something I could demand.

I'd already been delivered a toothbrush for $2. I looked through all the bathroom freebies. Shower gel, perfumed body lotion, perfumed dusting powder, sparkling foam bath, hair shampoo. That's what it said, "hair shampoo." What other kind of shampoo did they think I would take it for? Dog? Rug? Once in a Philadelphia hotel I found both "French milled bath soap" and "French milled personal soap." Accustomed as I am to doing personal things with my bath soap, I could not grasp the distinction and was afraid to ask. To this day I don't know whether there are things I do with bath soap that I shouldn't, at least in Philadelphia, or whether there are things that people do with soap in Philadelphia that I don't know about.

I sat there eating the last finger sandwich (I forgot to mention that we got a dozen of them for $15 and incidentals, and that they weren't tasty), wondering whether there were laws of room service I didn't know about. Deep-set principles that would of course have been ingrained in the young Elizabeth Taylor by MGM but that I missed out on, having been brought up in the Methodist . . .

It hit me what was missing here. I sprang to the phone, dialed 3.

"No Bible," I said.

"Sir?"

"I have been in and out of hotel rooms all over this nation, and I never thought I'd stumble into one with no Bible. What if I were Ollie North?"

The voice went away to check. "I'm sorry," it said in a moment. "There is not a Bible in the whole hotel."

"Oh. Well, then, can I have a pedicure? I'm going to confess something to you: I have never had a pedicure."

"Sir, it is too late."

The next morning I had eggs scrambled with too-pithy asparagus. A Czech manicurist came up and spent an hour on Christabel's fingernails and let her keep the bottle of polish. (If I'd known she was going to do that, we could have asked for yellow and used the extra to cover rust spots on the car.) I was delighted to find buttermilk on the menu, but dismayed to learn, when breakfast arrived, that there was no buttermilk in the hotel.

No oysters, no Bible, no buttermilk.

No wonder that the entire bill for our eighteen-hour stay, including the room and two local phone calls, came to only

$1,439.18. Less $2 for the buttermilk, which the woman at the front desk deducted after going back to the kitchen to make sure that I had, as I maintained, been charged for buttermilk. Add $35 for the manicure and $25 for various tips. Total outlays: $1,497.18, of which only $1, 073.40 could be construed as room service.

I don't know how Taylor does it. Of course she would not be too shy, as I was, to ask for a pedicure in broad daylight. And for her, someone would probably run round to the nearest Ramada Inn or after-hours Gideons International outlet for a Bible, and to her that's probably worth an extra $1,300 or so. But *every day?*

WHY I SMELL LIKE THIS

I burst into the last place on earth where I would go willingly—the men's fragrance department in Bloomingdale's—exclaiming, "I want to smell better."

Which was a lie.

The Board Room is what Bloomingdale's calls the place where it pushes men's aromas: a confined passage maybe ten yards long and three yards wide between two counters, with a little alcove in one corner. The walls and ceiling are chrome and black. Hanging on the walls are photographs of fragrances. Fragrances—men's, especially—are hard to capture visually. Several of these photographs show blown-up decanterlike bottles, bottles looking heavy enough to brain intruders with, yet bottles that glow. Bottles containing dynamic, masculine fragrances. Some of their names: Grey Flannel. Gruene. Quorum. Entrepreneur.

Rife—not to mention ripe—as this areaway is with scent, it seems even rifer, both behind and in front of the counters, with salespersons. Watching your movements. Making eye contact. Saying, "Citrus, of course. And black pepper. With a base of musk." Or, "Can I borrow your nose?"

I say "watching your movements," but I assume you have never been there. Who would go there? What was I doing there? I have a dynamic, masculine explanation. The only conceivable one.

I was scared.

Unless fear has an odor, I felt I smelled okay. Generally, all I feel I need to keep me fresh enough is baking soda. Some kind of product with baking soda in it. There is this toothpaste I have been able to find only in the South and the Midwest, called Peak, that has baking soda in it, and there is Shower to Shower body powder, which has baking soda and cornstarch in it.

I am not a shill for the baking soda and cornstarch industries. I am just saying these things meet my needs. So far as I can tell. And who wants to dwell too much on how he smells?

I have no business being in a store such as Bloomingdale's. It is not my scene. It makes me exude a slow, clinging, heavier-than-liquid sweat. But I went there out of the kindness of my heart, to buy a present. I was . . . shopping.

Once I met a woman who, in filling out a form for a computer dating service, had put down under hobbies, "Shopping and crying."

I am not like that. I will cry if I have to, but I would rather not, and I am the same way about shopping.

Well, I like to shop for groceries, because you don't have to try on groceries. And in grocery stores, they don't squirt things on you. They don't run out at you, shouting, "Here! Here! wouldn't you like some of this cheese stuff on your tongue?"

Bloomingdale's is so intense. There are so many people in there who—you can tell by the looks on their faces—promised themselves that they wouldn't go in there. Promised themselves, their parents, their spouses, their accountants: They wouldn't go in there for the rest of the month, at least. But there they are, again, driven by mindless need. They are shopping. And when they get home, they will cry.

And while they are in Bloomingdale's, they are being called to by sirens. People of both sexes line the aisles, brandishing hot-on-the-market unguents, emollients, wrinkle erasers, aura enhancers, antistaleness agents, musk elicitors, liquid talcs, essences of black orchid and teak.

And these sirens are not content just to tout their products. They try to get some on you. The air is full of their sprays, and if they can get ahold of your hand, they will squeeze creams out onto it.

And the names of these products! Niosôme. You know what Niosôme is? It is, according to a leaflet that was thrust into my hands, "beyond a cream or a lotion to a first-of-its-kind système." It is "a complex of . . . microscopic, multilayered spheres that are totally unique in their composition and action. In a phenomenon called biomimitism, these spheres mimic the skin's intercellular support organization."

Do you want a phenomenon like that going on, on your skin?

And what does the word "niosôme" (if "word" is the word for it) look like, at first, to you? To me, it looks like "noisome."

They give these products offensive-looking names! They make you think. Perhaps *I'm* noisome!

"Why don't you try some B.O.?" said one of the six or eight or ten salespersons in Bloomingdale's men's fragrance department, which, as I have said, is called the Board Room.

"What? You're going to spray *body odor* on me? *Whose?*" I cried.

"No, no," said the salesperson. "*V.O.*"

"Whiskey? You're going to spray whiskey on me?"

"No, no. V.O. Eau de Toilette Homme." V.O. stands for Version Originale.

It's all foreign names in these tony smell parlors, you know. You don't see your basic green American skin bracers; you see things named for princesses, and I don't mean Fergie. I thought exotic princesses spent their time trying not to get caught on mattresses with peas under them, but no, not today! Today, they crank out effluvia for men!

You think I was oversensitive to this V.O. reference? You think I'm leaping to the conclusion that fragrance names seek to evoke *fear*?

Okay, then, why was there a beautiful woman standing in a

Bloomingdale's aisle under a sign that said "POISON"? Poison! She was standing there trying to put Poison on people and then looking cranky when they didn't buy some!

"Poison?" I said to her.

"No, no," she said semi-indulgently. *"Pwa-zawnh.* It is French." And she showed me on the sample that she was trying to get within squirting distance of my wrist: "NEW POISON CRÈME SOMPTUEUSE."

"Are you sure that's right?" I asked. "Are you sure it's not supposed to be spelled *poisson,* which I happen to know means 'fish'?"

"No, no," she said less indulgently. *"Pwa-zawnh.* It is a French word meaning 'beautiful woman.' "

"I see," I said. A dab of it had appeared on the back of my hand. It smelled all right, I guess, but it looked like bird-doo.

"Rub it in," she urged.

I ran. Because I was desperate. Poison wasn't enough, I needed something stronger. And that is how I found myself in the Board Room.

Where, as I say, there must have been at least eight salespersons behind the counters. And each of them wanted to spray me with something. And I let them! I even sprayed things on myself! Eight, ten, twelve different things, containing cardamom, galbanum, *lavande, bois de rose, moussse de chêne, cannelle,* cumin, patchouli, geranium, wood notes, leather, tobacco, oak moss, and citrus.

And vanilla. Do you know those ads in which several people are pictured in a grainy naked heap, always with an extra leg or so that you can't quite tell the sex or owner of? Those ads for . . . that's right: Obsession. (Why would something called Obsession *need* to advertise?) Well, there is Obsession fragrance, which laces all manner of creams and splashes, and then there is Obsession for Men, which aromatizes balms (a balm called Obsession?) and all sorts of "body products" (I'll tell you what's a body product: sweat) for men. Often, today's women, according to the salespersons in the Board Room, prefer Obsession for Men. And do you know what the difference between Obsession and Obsession for Men is? According to one of those salespersons?

Obsession for Men has less vanilla in it.

Vanilla! Now, I have heard of people (not tony people, though) *drinking* vanilla extract and then doing things they felt sheepish about afterward, but I have never heard of anyone being swept up into disorienting activity by the *smell* of vanilla.

But did I spray on myself or allow to be sprayed on myself Obsession and countless other men's fragrances? Yes. Not only that, but I kept sniffing at myself, all up and down both forearms. And I smelled salespersons' arms! "Here, smell me," a salesman said. "It's already mellowed out on my skin."

I was smelling a strange guy's arm!

I even bought things! At $25, $35 per bottle, and let me tell you, those bottles aren't as big as they look in the photographs, thank God. Things that, when I smelled them, it was like biting into strange new pickles: I had no way of knowing whether they had gone bad or not. I had to buy them, because the Board Room does not take kindly to fragrance leeches. The salespersons seem to sniff them out. A harmless old guy in a safari jacket came through while I was there, cadging spritzes and trying to talk to people in either French or German about his experiences in Europe during the Second World War, and since he did not buy anything, he was discouraged from lingering.

I had to linger. I had to take on all the fragrances I could.

For this reason. The only possible honorable reason.

Here's what happened.

Shortly after I'd entered Bloomingdale's, I'd dropped some change and bent over to pick it up. And you know how sometimes you're backed up farther against a counter or something than you realize, so when you stand up, your behind hits the counter or whatever at a certain angle and you pitch forward suddenly?

That happened to me, and it caused me to tackle this guy. Inadvertently. I'd never seen him before in my life. Why would anyone tackle a complete stranger in Bloomingdale's?

That's what made it look so bad. Well, that was one of the things.

The guy was lying in the aisle, outraged. And he was swarthy, wore sunglasses, and was huge. Weight-lifter arms and shoulders, in this tank top.

And his nose curled as I disengaged (I had some beer and Vietnamese fish sauce on me from lunch, and some spot remover from just after breakfast, and I was sweating), and he shouted, "I'll get you, you son of a bitch! You'll never get out of this store alive! I'd recognize you anywhere!"

And he was blind.

MY PLACE AMONG THE FOUNDING FATHERS

When slavery was discusssed at the Constitutional Convention, John Rutledge of South Carolina said that "religion and humanity" were not on the table. "Interest alone," he said, "is the governing principle with nations."

So if I could go back in time and serve as a delegate, I would advance my interest. As the only Deep Southern member of the Massachusetts delegation, I would depend on neither slavery nor Calvinism for my life-style—and would, therefore, enjoy a pretty free hand. Also I would have the advantage of knowing how all this was going to look in two hundred years.

If I played my cards right, I'd have a good shot to get into Bartlett's *Familiar Quotations*—before I was born. Think how that would have looked on my college applications.

Here are some of the famous things I would say:

• "Every American at times will favor a strict interpretation of this Constitution, at times a loose. It will depend. On who is trying to get away with what. This will be a very dependable Constitution."

• "I believe this government cannot endure permanently half slave and half free." (Getting in ahead of Abe.)

• "I take it that what we really mean by this first part is 'We, the men.' A time will come, gentlemen, when that won't wash."

Just think what moral capital that last saying would afford me now, in interaction with today. At the time, of course, it would shake up the convention. Hey, somebody's got to be the loose cannon. I could accuse the other delegates of not knowing how to act around women. James Madison, I understand, was so shy in their presence (Dolley, eventually, being the exception) that a woman described him as "the most unsociable creature in existence."

In fact, Madison was shy with just about everyone. History tells us that someone once reached through the window of an inn where he was stopping and stole his hat. This made Madison feel so naked that he stayed off the streets for two days, until he managed to buy a hat from a passing snuff dealer (one with, presumably, a small head, for Madison was diminutive). Think of the strategems I could pull on Madison—slipping into the cloak-room every day and replacing his hat with one that looked just like it, but each day was a half-size larger.

I would only do such a thing for a purpose. After a week or so, I would take him aside and offer to tell him how to stop his head from shrinking, if he would throw his weight behind my proposal to grant slaves the right to incorporate themselves over a period of time through the accumulation of sweat equity.

Why is it in my interest to make a two-hundred-year-old antislavery name for myself? Well, I grew up as a white male Georgian, having to prove that I was not on the wrong side of everything. It took a lot out of me.

So at the convention, I would make observations like: "I gather, then, that we are holding as self-evident the truth that all men are created equal until someone kidnaps and sells them."

"Who *is* this bird?" the other delegates would be muttering.

"What they say in Massachusetts is, he's crazy but he gets away with it because he's so *prescient*. He even called Shays' Rebellion."

"Also, he's got so many jokes and sayings that no one has

heard. Did you hear him yesterday? 'Candy is dandy, but liquor is quicker.' "

"And Washington likes him."

Here's the reason Washington would like me: He would have listened enthralled one evening in Mount Vernon as I told him about the George Washington Bridge, George Washington University, the *Washington Post,* the Washington Redskins, the Washington Square Bar and Grill, the Washington Monument, and the state of Washington.

I would also fill Washington in on George Washington Carver, Booker T. Washington, Dinah Washington, Harold Washington, Grover Washington, Jr., Kermit Washington, and Claudell Washington. "And will there be no accomplished . . . *white* people named Washington?" he would have wondered, and I would have said, "I can't think of any."

"There will arise a man named Kareem Abdul-Jabbar," I would tell the assembled delegates, "and you needn't think, whatever is decided here, that he will be only three fifths as tall." The notion of Jabbar would disquiet Madison particularly, considering how easily someone seven foot four could steal a short statesman's hat.

"I notice that we are referring to slaves as 'Other Persons,' " I would tell the convention. "It may interest you to learn that two centuries from now, the most valuable commodity in America will be Other Persons' Money."

Which leads us to a touchy point: whether I would make money out of my constitutional connection. My problem there is that I am not much of a businessman. Someone else in my position might come up with a way to license the expression "What the Founding Fathers had in mind," but that is not the kind of thing I am good at.

No, in order to get rich off the convention I would have to involve my relative—William Blount, a delegate from North Carolina. And I hate to do that because of the sleaze factor. My historical standing would suffer, if I could be tarred by the same brush as my relative.

Indeed, one reason I would welcome the chance to be a delegate would be to take some of the taint off the family name. Among the delegates, say Christopher Collier and James Lincoln Collier in their book *Decision in Philadelphia,* there was "at least one outright scoundrel, William Blount." Nor do they leave it at that. "It is worth noting," they go on to say, "that there is no record of Blount's ever having said anything at the convention. He thus becomes the exception that proves the rule: even this dishonorable man was sufficiently awed by the historical importance of the event to keep his mouth shut and eschew his usual rascality."

In *The Natural Superiority of Southern Politicians* (a respectable book, whatever you may leap to infer from the title), David Leon Chandler is kinder: "If Jefferson's life encompassed the noble and lofty aspects of the Southern character, then William Blount illustrates the common clay, the ambitious frontiersmen and land-grabbers who put together the western wing of the Deep South."

William is not my linear ancestor, but he was one of the first bunch of Blounts in America, which is the bunch from which I derive, and what you can say about that bunch is that they loved real estate. William had such a craving for it ("there is a continent for sale," he said in a letter) that in 1797 he tried to protect his investments by means of, well, treason—more specifically, unauthorized dealings with what might be called, in the phrase often heard in the Iran-Contra investigations, a third nation.

By this time, he had moved to Tennessee, bought a great deal of it, and become its first governor and then one of its U.S. senators. Concerned that his Western holdings were threatened by the Spanish, he conspired with the British to mount an attack on Spanish-held Pensacola and New Orleans. Word got out. Britgate. Blount was impeached and expelled from the Senate.

Maybe I could have warned him. But I doubt it. Blount acted according to his own antennae. And he came out of his -gate pretty well. The folks back in Tennessee never lost faith in him. He died ensconced in the state senate, and his mansion in Knoxville still stands.

Here is something I might consider advocating, as a delegate to the convention: setting up a Department of Scandal, or even a whole House of Scandal. Why not institutionalize scandal? Too much time is lost, under the present system, in appointing Congessional panels and independent counsels. Let's have a standing -gate program, ready to go on public TV at a week's notice.

But no, that would not be for a Blount to propose, at least not in the eighteenth century. My best bet at the convention would be to distance myself from my distinguished relative.

Of course, my efforts in that direction might go less smoothly than I have been imagining. Blount would be whispering in my ear every so often, "This is off the record, but I want you to talk to a few of the boys. I see a way we can control half the action in Louisiana." And Madison might be hard to take down a peg. He might keep his hat next to him at all times. If a couple of my jibes should misfire, history might . . . in fact, *I* might be awed by the historical importance of the event.

Wait a minute. You don't suppose I *was* William Blount?

I *DON'T EAT DIRT PERSONALLY*

When we read items in the *New York Times* about human behavior or the physical universe or so on, our reaction is, "Well, this is certainly On Solid Ground." Not long ago the *Times* revealed . . . that scientists had disovered . . . that people who were told not to think about a white bear had a lot more thoughts about a white bear than people who weren't told not to think about a white bear. I forget the exact figures. Any day I expect the *Times* to disclose research establishing that some strikingly low percentage of people know you when you're down and out.

So when the *Times* runs something that reflects on me as a Southerner, I can't just dismiss it as off the wall. I have to explain it to the people I live among, which is to say Northerners. One morning I picked up the *Times* and saw my work cut out for me. Here was the headline: SOUTHERN PRACTICE OF EATING DIRT SHOWS SIGNS OF WANING.

"While it is not uncommon these days to find people here who eat dirt," the story said, many Southerners "are giving up dirt because of the social stigma attached to it."

Now, I would be willing to argue, in a quasi-agrarian way, that the giving up of dirt is part of the downside of modern life. The giving up of eating dirt, however, is a subject that I frankly kind of resent having to discuss. And not because it hits too close to home. The truth is, I never started eating dirt. The stigma attached to dirt-eating is one of a handful of stigmas that I have never even considered feeling. But try telling that to Northerners.

People who attend fashionable Northern soirées read the *New York Times*. The very night of the dirt-eating story, I was in someone's chic salon eating arugula. A woman with a crewcut heard my accent.

"What do you do?" she asked.

I said I was a writer.

"Ah, yes," she said. "Of course. Southerners are all natural storytellers. Sitting on the old screen porch, dog under the rocker, flies on the baby, everyone spitting and spinning yarns compounded of biblical cadences and allusions to animals named B'rer.

"One thing I never realized, though," she went on, "was that you eat dirt."

At that point there were two tacks I could take. I could say, "Well, I know there are some folks down South who like to chew on clay, but I never ate any myself and neither did any of my relatives or friends, and in point of fact I never even saw anybody eat dirt."

The response to that tack would have been a knowing look. "Here is a man who comes from people who eat dirt and he thinks he is better than they are." She would be thinking I couldn't handle stigma. Or that I was inauthentic. Southern *and* inauthentic: the worst of both worlds.

So I took the second tack. "Hell, yes, we eat dirt," I said. "And if you never ate any blackened red dirt, you don't know what's good. I understand you people up here eat raw fish."

You know how sushi got started, don't you? Some Tokyo marketing people were sitting around thinking how they could create a whole new American market, and one of them said, "Restaurants."

And another one said, "Okay. What would these restaurants serve?"

"Oh, fish."

"What would be the most cost-effective way of cooking it?" asked another.

And the eyes of another one lit up, and he said, "You know what we could do . . . ?"

But of course sushi was dead now, I told this Northerner, and people were Cajuned out, and even New Zealand cuisine was about to go the way of Australian, and now this hot New Guinea place, Yam Yam, was so overpraised, I figured the time was ripe for investing in dirt restaurants.

None of the Northerners I used this tack on had realized that it was time to be Cajuned out, even. The best way to get a Northerner to believe something is to talk to him as if you assume that he knows it already and that most people don't. I raised $3,800 in one evening. I figured when these investors came to me wondering what had happened to their money, I could admit that dirt-dining wasn't quite happening yet after all—that when they had invested in it, it had been ahead of its time. Which would have consoled them more than you might think.

Then the *Times* came out with another headline: "QUIET CLAY REVEALED AS VIBRANT AND PRIMAL." According to some scientists, the first forms of life may have begun in clay. This was too close to what I learned as a boy back in Sunday school for comfort. And I didn't want to be explaining why Southerners eat life at its very source. But then I thought, what the heck. "Yep," I told Northerners at parties. "In fact, if there'd been a Southerner around at the time when the first forms of life were getting underway, he'd've been nipped in the mud." People who weren't put off by raw fish were certainly not dismayed to learn that dirt was, in a sense, their mother.

The *third* dirt-related *Times* headline was the one that made my position difficult. CLAY EATING PROVES WIDESPREAD BUT REASON IS UNCERTAIN, it said.

"Uh-oh," I thought, and I was right.

"The practice of eating dirt, usually fine clays, is so common in so many societies," the *Times* story began, "that it must be regarded as a normal human behavior rather than an oddity, according to scientists who are studying it."

Dirt-eating, the *Times* had now decided, was known by experts as geophagy, and was no more peculiarly Southern—or, for that matter, peculiar—than rabbits. "Historical records of earth-eating in Europe go back to 300 B.C., when Aristotle described it," said the newspaper of record.

And the Northerners wanted their money back. Some of them had reached the conclusion that there was no real prestige value in dirt. Others wanted to look into importing as-yet-underpriced French dirts. I told them I had plowed all their money into development.

What I had done was send the money to my Uncle Mullet, who did eat dirt. When I said I never had any relative who ate dirt, I wasn't counting my Uncle Mullet, who is not my blood uncle and I never felt responsible for him, because he did everything, up to and including worship through snakebite. He wasn't typical of anybody's family. He kept armadillos and lived with a woman named Valvoline. He always did just exactly what nobody wanted him to, and wouldn't even talk to anybody else in the family on the phone. Didn't have a phone. So no wonder I would feel free to say that I never had any relatives who ate dirt.

But Uncle Mullet did, and one afternoon he went over to his favorite clayhole to dig some up, and a man dressed all in freshly-ordered-looking L. L. Bean clothing came out from behind a tree to wave a POSTED sign at him.

"Stranger," the man said in a northern accent, "you are eating my land."

"What do you mean, *'stranger'*?" my Uncle Mullet said. "I been coming here for generations."

The Northerner looked at him in a certain way.

"What do you mean, *'your land'*?"my Uncle Mullet said. "This spot has been free for folks to come to for clay ever since I don't know when."

The Northerner looked at him a certain way.

"And what do you mean, *'eating'*?" Uncle Mullet said. "I wouldn't . . ."

And that's what broke his spirit. After a lifetime of doing every awful thing he felt like, proudly, Uncle Mullet had denied to a Northerner that he did something that he had always done. Had denied it just because the Northerner had looked at him in a certain way enough times to make him feel looked at in a certain way.

And it disgusted Uncle Mullet to the point that he stopped trying to shift for himself, and everybody in the family had to start sending my Aunt Rayanne money to keep him up. (Valvoline dropped him.)

And of course the reason the man in the unbroken-in L. L. Bean outfit was protecting the old clayhole was that he had just bought all that area through there so he could get in on the ground floor of the chain of fine dirt restaurants that I had led him to believe, late one night in that chic salon, was about to happen.

We reap what we sow.

A VERSE TO THE NEW SOUTH

Yes, bartender, I'll have anuthun,
And yes, reader, I am a Suthun
Writer. One who knows about Dixie—
Where I haven't lived since Sixie-
Eight. I know its rocks and rills, though,
And, God knows, its ills, though
Come to think of it, maybe I don't
Anymore. My shifty oppon't,
Displacement, has me pinned up North,
Because of my life and so forth
And so on. ("Nawth," I'm aware,
Doesn't rhyme with "fo'th." There
Are still some things that I'm on top of.
And every year I grow a crop of
Collard greens, which *like* cold weather.)

Well. It's nice to get together
With a Southern audience.
People who have got some sense.
Here is what my topic is:
Even though the New South's riz,
The South's the South.

People say:
"TV finished what TVA
Began. It turned the South into

Just another part of New
Nowhere, wired into the Feddle
Government and other meddle-
Some blandifying forces which
Knock Southernness right in the ditch.
The South today's like anywhere else
Where money talks and butter melts,
Except that [save in some folks' mouth]
Butter melts faster in the South.
The world is all one Global Village,
A rainbow slick of techno-spillage.
Everything's new, and pretty soon
The *Earth*'ll be South, because the moon
Will be up where wiseguys hang out.
Who *cares* anymore what 'the South' is about?"

That kind of talk makes me lose patience.
Are Seminoles just non-French-speaking Haitians?
Are rich Alabamans the same as Kuwaitis?
Peachtree Creek just a branch of the Eighties?

No. I don't believe it. No.
If you think so, then you should go
To Haiti or Kuwait and see.
The South is still the South to me.
Compared to, say, the North, at least.
Not to mention the West and East.

Maybe the recent Cracker Presidency
Was largely characterized by hesitancy—
Still, I thought its yell was Rebel.
Just should've been pitched a bit less treble.
Carter *could*'ve used fresher grease,
But I'll take Lance if you'll take Meese.

There's Southern new and Northern new,
And one is warmer and funkier too,
And one has no fried okra at all.
And I know which, and so do y'all.

The question: Is there any theah theah
In the South? My answer: yeah.

HAVING WONDERFUL TIME SUCKLING LITTLE DOG

. . . . . .

The best postcard is the one that makes you think, "Aha! This one showing all but the head of a seated woman holding an enormous constrained-but-unruffled-looking gray rabbit in her lap or, rather, between her attractively crossed legs, in an odd attitude and feeding it an outsized carrot, which the rabbit seems not to relish, is just right for . . ." Actually that card is not just right for anyone, which is why I still have it. It has no caption. I got it in France, years ago, and for some reason it reminds me of a beautiful Frenchwoman with whom I grilled sausages out in the woods. She said something half in English, half in French about how I must be accustomed to fancier outings, being an American. *"Je suis ordinaire,"* I assured her. Momentarily, and inopportunely, that Frenchwoman turned my head, partly because it was so hard to figure out what she was saying. You know what I mean? I love the Maigret mysteries because I am so proud of myself for solving the French. I am reluctant to read one in English because of the element of bafflement that would be lost. France is a good place for a *certain kind* of postcard.

In England, the best cards are the traditional type, about which George Orwell wrote: "Your first impression is of overpowering vulgarity. . . . Your second impression, however, is of indefinable familiarity."

A staple of these cards is the overheard remark. Husband hanging up his coat and hat at home hears a man's voice saying to his shapely wife (who is just out of his sight, answering the door), "Where would you like it, missus—on the carpet or on the edge of the table?" The man at the door is of course the postman, with a package. But the husband doesn't know that.

Room-service man walking past the (inexplicably open) door of a room in a "honeymoon hotel" hears the groom saying, "Shall I let it go—or catch it in my nightshirt?" The groom is of course talking about a mouse, which has caused his curvaceous bride to jump up onto a chair. He is standing over the mouse, holding the nightshirt in question. But the room-service man doesn't know that.

I am willing to bet—I am not saying this lightly—that the course of my life has been changed regrettably, over and over, by just such innocent remarks. Made by me, heard by me, or heard by someone I loved. If only I could trace my steps back over each such remark, reclaim and clarify each such moment for everyone involved, including me. . . .

Life is too short. What I can do is mail postcards, in the hope that they will bring into somewhat sharper focus the confusions of the road. From Jerry's Shell Mini-Market in Cornersville, Tennessee: a man (outside a bar) lying on his side on some boards on the ground, scrabbling around grimly and saying, "I'll climb this fence if it takes me all night!"

I can't claim to be a postcard collector, but I do have an "Unnatural Nursing" file:

"Dog as Foster Mother to Baby Lions, Lincoln Park, Chicago."

"A Mule Giving Milk to a Calf, McLean, Texas."

"Indian Woman Suckling a Little Dog—Venezuela."

I have not gone out looking for these pictures of creatures imbibing strange maternal juices—I just came upon them here and there. Maybe it's something psychological on my part. But let me say this: I showed this file to my friend Sandy Frazier (author of *Dating Your Mom*) the other night, and he said *he* had a card of a woman nursing a human baby on one side and a bear cub on the other.

I have the card that a certain Addie sent a certain Mrs. Lillian Goodemote in 1912. A couple is shown smooching, both their heads concealed by the lady's hat, under the caption "Hidden opportunities in Gowanda, N.Y." Here is what Addie wrote:

"I will answer your easter card now and you was right when you said no one thought of me now for your card was all the one I received are all well hope you are the same have been working down town or would of ritten sooner."

Some name, Mrs. Goodemote. Wonder what she wrote back. "No no I did not mean to say you was not thought of by many what I ment was . . ."? No, I don't think people generally explained themselves in that way, back then.

Or even in 1928, when some English child received a postcard portraying (fearsomely, with billowing black smoke covering most of the photograph) "Guns of H.M.S. *Renown* in action." The caption on the back: "These guns throw projectiles weighing about 1,900 lbs. each, so that the total weight of the shells of a double salvo is about 3½ tons. Effective range 20 miles. Muzzle velocity 2,650 ft. per second. Shell will penetrate 57.5 inches of wrought iron. . . ." And this personal note: "Aren't these big guns? Love, Mummie."

Postcards reveal changes in mores. For years I took for granted that it would be a woman whose bikinied behind an alligator was about to bite in those "Us Alligators are having fun in Florida" cards. Now I have found a card in which the about-to-be-nipped bathing beauty is a man. Uh-oh.

"I like the old postcards that have a man standing there next to things. To show what size they are," said my friend Lee Smith, author of *Family Linen,* recently. "I feel reassured by that man."

It's not always the same man, though, I mentioned.

"Well no, that wouldn't be possible," she said.

Certainly it's not a job I would want to take on myself, I said. But then I stopped to think.

Wouldn't I have enjoyed being the man perched right inside the cut-away forehead of *S. Carlo in Arona, Statua più colossale del mondo,* which I assume means "Saint Carlo in Arona, the most colossal statue of the world." Or the woman dwarfed by the "44-POUND CABBAGE grown near Palmer in the fertile Matanuska Valley, Alaska." You should see this cabbage. (No trick photography. I won't even go into the cards I have of gigantic joke cabbages, grasshoppers, potatoes, rabbits.) The poundage isn't the half of it. In fact, I would have said the cabbage weighed more than the woman. If I had been this woman, I would be able to speak with authority about this cabbage's scope; as it is, I can only look at the postcard and tell you that, in my estimation, this is a cabbage you could get lost in.

Oh, I could go on and on about postcards. Cards with cotton bolls stapled to them, cards of ducklings or bathing beauties that squeak when squeezed, 3-D cards in which Jesus (or a Japanese girl's underwear) fades in and out, cards with odd prose:

"Texas longhorn. This various type has been world known."

"East Subsistance and Lean Too's, New Fort Lyon, Colo."

Some cards tell more about the place they celebrate than they mean to. Fifteen years ago I found a card in Birmingham that displayed a modest brick house with the caption "Beautiful Negro homes." Birmingham could boast quite a few Negroes who kept up nice houses, the card said on the back. There were no people in the photograph.

No one, I believe, could argue with what is printed on the back of an otherwise indistinct card I have from Niagara Falls:

"This view of the falls must be seen to be properly appreciated."

But I prefer cards to vistas. Cards are man-made—so more mysterious. And you can write on them. I have one from Sandy Frazier showing "Paisano Pete/World's Largest Roadrunner/Ft. Stockton, Texas." Pete is a statue. There is no one standing next to him, but the card says he is twenty feet long. On the card, about the card, Sandy has written:

"The woman . . . where I bought it was on the telephone when I came to the counter. She said, 'You say you want our marriage to work, and you're out runnin' around? Shit!' (then, to me) 'Will that be all for you?' "

I CAN'T PLAY GOLF

It is a source of confusion and embarrassment to me that I am just now writing about my participation in the Chet Atkins Country Gentleman Celebrity Golf Tournament, which was held at Callaway Gardens in Pine Mountain, Georgia.

It has taken this long for the experience to sink in, or hole out (I can never get golf terms straight). The truth is, the tournament itself was a source of confusion and embarrassment to me. Of course, so is life.

But at least in life I don't get into the wrong golf cart.

At the Chet Atkins Country Gentleman Celebrity Golf Tournament, I did that several times. Got into the wrong golf cart. Used the wrong club. Hit the ball off into the woods where everybody had to help me find it, and then sat down in somebody else's golf cart. Also put my clubs in the wrong . . . what do you call it? *Bag.* I knew that. The wrong bag. I think that's how I lost a three-wood. I understand it's fairly common to lose a wedge, but a three-wood, no.

I told Chet, when he called to invite me, "Chet I'd be proud to be in your tournament, but I can't play golf."

A simple, strightforward statement: "I can't play golf."

Nobody ever believes it. It's like "I can't sing." Nobody believes it until you show them.

So I went down to Callaway Gardens, and they asked me

what my handicap was. I said, "I can't play golf." And they laughed and sat there with their pencils poised, and I said, "Well, if you want me to narrow it down any more than that, I guess I will soon enough." And I did. Right out there on the course. I found out what my handicap was. It was 86. Not counting water.

But first I met my four partners. I told them, "Hi, howdy, hey, nice to meet you. I can't play golf."

And they chuckled. Thought I was hustling them, I guess. I mean, there I was, with my Chet Atkins Country Gentleman Celebrity Golf Tournament visor and my Chet Atkins Country Gentleman Celebrity Golf Tournament shirt and my white golf shoes. I had bought the white golf shoes at the pro shop. With black rubber cleats, not metal spikes. I figured, where will I ever wear shoes with metal nails sticking out of them? Whereas I might be able to wear white shoes with black rubber cleats to a reception, or something.

I guess my group thought I was blowing smoke. But no, I was telling the truth. I couldn't play golf. Not only that, but I never had played golf. Well, I had played miniature golf, and I had hit buckets of balls at driving ranges.

I can drive some, as long as I'm on a rubber mat, and I can putt some, as long as they haven't got the windmill set up too fast, but in between I might as well hold the ball between my feet and advance it by a series of hops as try to hit it any given distance in any given direction with any given iron.

And I hate to let on. I mean, I will make a basic statement up front: "I can't play golf." But when it comes to specifics, well . . . As I am lining up to take a particular shot, something keeps me from being candid enough to start hollering, "Have mercy! Somebody! Help me! I ain't got the first earthly idea which one of those things to pull out of that bag, and I don't know what to do with it once I do pull it out! And I don't know the way back to the clubhouse!"

So I chose a couple of sticks at random and took a couple of whacks on the same principle, and my partners said without hesitation, "It's true. You can't play golf."

And I said, "I told you. I told Chet. But . . ."

And they said, "Well, uh, why would you pay all the money to come all the way down here to play golf, then, if you can't play golf?"

And I said, "Well, actually . . . I'm one of the . . . in fact, I am this foursome's . . . um, celebrity."

And they said, "Oh." (I think they had been looking around at each other, wondering which one of us was.) "Who are you?"

It is hard to think of an excuse for not being famous enough. "Well, I haven't been feeling too well lately." Or, "Wait till I've had a couple of drinks." Or, "Well, I used to be more famous than this, but it was a strange thing, they say statistically it was almost unheard of, but in one day last year, 85 percent of the people in America who had heard of me all died in car wrecks."

There ought to be some kind of handicap for triple-bogey celebrities. If you'd spot me an Emmy, a Grammy and a *People* cover, say, I could be on a recognition par with nearly any of the other celebs who played in Chet's tournament: James Garner, Johnny Bench, Ray Stevens, Claude Akins, Archie Campbell, Billy Edd Wheeler, any of them. (Another entertainment figure was penciled in, but he called ahead of time and said he'd just had a new hairpiece fitted, and if it worked out he was going to go on tour. And I guess it did.)

But nobody wants to go back home from a celebrity tournament and tell people, "You know who I played golf with? This old boy named Ray Blump or something, who, if he'd ever been married to Madonna and kidnapped by terrorists and named to the U.S. Supreme Court, would be as famous as you please."

So I just had to go with my poor fame and poor game that had got me there. "You've got a good swing," a club pro named Danny Berrier from Knoxville, Tennessee, told me. "You've got the worst grip I've ever seen and the worst address I've ever seen, and you've got the worst backswing I've ever seen, and you've got shoes on that cause you to shift forward a couple of inches as you come through, but you've got a good swing."

I wound up not playing very well at all. What I was able to do, though, was this: I fell back on country music. I decided, as I trod the out-of-bounds trying to find the people who were trying to help me find my ball, that I could ease my misery by expressing it in terms of country songs.

A lot of people don't associate country music with golf. But Willie Nelson has his own course, where the rules include:

• No more than twelve to a foursome.
• Par is how you feel that day.
• No change-jingling or wind-letting on the greens.
• USGA rules apply except where you can think of something better.
• If you land in some rocks, you can pick your ball up and walk it over to the grass. This is called "putting the Pedernales Stroll on it."

And more pertinently, Chet Atkins is country music's premier guitar player, father of the Nashville Sound and a member of the Country Music Hall of Fame. Ray Stevens, Archie Campbell, and Billy Edd Wheeler are big country music figures. Billy Edd Wheeler wrote "Jackson." And Johnny Bench can sing any song Ray Stevens ever wrote. If it had been the Zubin Mehta Celebrity Golf Classic, I might have been out of luck. But country music has helped me through a great many crises. Either by making me feel better or by making me feel so much worse that it was fascinating.

I'll tell you what I started doing there at Callaway Gardens last September and have been doing since.

First, I thought of all the country song titles that might be about golf:

"Born to Lose"
"Crazy Arms"
"Dang Me"

"Don't Let Me Cross Over"
"Eight More Miles to Louisville"
"Green, Green Grass of Home"
"Headin' Down the Wrong Highway"
"I'm a Fool to Care"
"I Really Don't Want to Know"
"It Makes No Difference Now"
"There Goes My Everything"

And there's that line from "Nine Pound Hammer": "Roll on, buddy, don't you roll so slow."

My heart still hurt, though, when I had thought of all those things, so I started making up country-golf song titles:

"I Got No More Business in a Golf Tournament (Than You Do in My Heart)"
"I'm Just A-Tryin' to Hit a Straight Lick (with a Crooked Stick)"
"You Can't Tell My Heart from a Hole in the Ground"
"Like a Fool I Kept Giving You Mulligans (But You Didn't Want to Shoot Straight)"
"I Must Be Doing What I Did Before (Because I Seem to Be Doing It Again)"
"I Love It When You Pitch and Roll"

But titles weren't enough. I got to where I was thinking up lyrics:

Don't worry, dear, that I will stray.
My love continues true.
Each time I take a shot at her,
I slice right back to you.

Why won't you let me iron this out,
So we can get to kissin'?
I try and try to improve my lie,
But you just will not listen.

You got too many pigs snufflin'
At your trough:
The heck with you, I'll go play golf.

I'll never go 'round with you again,
You use the coarsest language.
I also didn't like it when
You hit me with your sand wedge.

Tell me why if you're so true
And full of gentle virtue,
My friends when I drive straight at you
Don't tell me, "That won't hurt you"?

I picture myself doing everything right,
But then I don't, by a looooong sight—
I don't see how I ever lose,
Yet here I quake in these spiked shoes.
I got the positive attitude blues.

Finally I got to where I was feeling golf so deeply that I wrote an entire song. Well, I nearly finished one called "I Think I'll Just Sleep in the Car," about a golfer who comes home too late, see, and he gets as far as his driveway. . . .

I'm drunk, the clock is striking four,
And there Lucille stands in the door.
The roll across our threshold there
Is hard to read. I do declare,
I hit my drive just perfect, but
I left myself a hell of a putt.

So I think I'll just sleep in the car,
Till I feel more up to par.
I think I'll just sleep in the car.

But I went all the way with this one, a whole heart-tugging ballad that I call "The Long Nineteenth." Let me say, incidentally, that if someone more famous than I am wants to cut a record of it, I will feel that my golf game has been redeemed. It goes kind of like this:

There's a mashie niblick rusting
In a water hazard deep
Because its master flung it there
Before he went to sleep.

And also there's a nine-iron,
A driver and a spoon—
Lying all unplayably
Beneath a slice of moon.

And look: There's sev'ral dozen
Golfballs, dusted o'er.
They miss the man by whom they were
So often shanked before.

But do not grieve, equipment.
The man who used to swear
And bury you beneath the sand
Is now pin-high somewhere.

He's gone on to the Big Clubhouse
Where golfers all wind up,
Where everywhere he lands is green,
An arm's length from the cup.

Ah, now he uses angels' tees.
His earthly game's surpassed.
He smiles at golf from up above:
His head is down at last.

And yet, after all this, I know I don't have enough experience in the sport to sing of it profoundly. You have to learn to play the game before you realize you will never learn to play it. That came home to me when I heard what James Garner—who is a three handicapper—remarked when he hit a ball perfectly onto one of those Callaway Gardens greens and for some reason, known only to the ball itself, it just kept on moving. Garner said: "One of 'em holds, and one of 'em rolls. And you never know which."

So, after thanking Chet for this opportunity to plunge myself into a new field of despair, I want to dedicate this last lyric to James Garner (who won my esteem on *Rockford Files* when he did a car chase all over a fancy golf course):

> *One of 'em holds and one of 'em rolls,*
> *And I never know which one is which.*
> *And that explains why I'm here all alone*
> *And also have never been rich.*

By the way, I call James Garner "Jim" now. Of course he . . .

Hey, now that's a song. "The Sort-of-Celebrity Duckhook Blues":

> *I call James Garner "Jim" now.*
> *Course, he calls me "Jim" too.*
> *Yes, I've played with him now,*
> *While he was playing through.*
>
> *He acted just as natural,*
> *And as for me, I tried.*
> *And Johnny Bench, the catcher'll*
> *Tell you how I cried:*
>
> *"Oh, I know that I'm a lot less*
> *Famous than you all,*
> *And I know that I'm not spotless*
> *When I try to stroke the ball.*

"So go on, wield your mashies
Well, and be well known.
I'll stay back where the trash is.
Go on. That's right. Go on.

"At least you know this morning
I wasn't crying wolf
When I gave you every warning
I never could play golf."

No LONGER OUT OF PLACE, NOT EVEN YOU

. . . . .

The key is how, and where, to fit in. To some this comes naturally, as we read in Liz Smith's column:

> Mrs. Astor's reason for turning down a party in the Palladium's Mike Todd Room? "Really, I don't think my friends would go to 14th St." On the other hand, there is no place in New York where Mrs. Astor won't go in a good cause, and recently she fell over a construction at the South Street Seaport and had to accept medical aid from some concerned workers.

For you, though, it has always been different. You are at a fête where you don't know anyone except your hostess—who, when you wave, gives you a look of . . . well, to call it consternation is to oversimplify: a narrowing of the eyes, followed by a widening, followed by another narrowing that very nearly amounts to a graciously modulated wince.

And you have forgotten to shave either one side of your face or one leg, as the case may be. And everyone else is wearing tennis togs, while you have come semiformal except for one of those funny caps that look like an animal's head. No one else is wearing anything jocular or any sort of cap.

Furthermore, what with the way you have been feeling for the past few weeks, you have neglected to keep abreast of anything, in or out of the news, except for your symptoms—most notably an odd cloggedness (and yet to say "cloggedness" is not to put it just right) in your sinuses.

You have spilled a whole banana margarita in your lap; something feels askew about your underwear; and you notice—in the reflection of someone's mirror sunglasses just before they are quickly averted—what looks like a lot of ball-point ink on your upper lip and nose.

How do you blend? How do you mingle?

Not by tripping over a construction. At this point, whatever you trip over will be regarded as something you have misconstrued.

So here's what you do.

"All right, everybody!" you announce. "Listen up. Enough about my hard-to-pin-down sinus condition—which is history now, anyway. It's about to be taken up by Eurotrash. I'm beginning to have trouble with something else, perhaps my sense of the Other. Have you had the feeling that your sense of the Other is getting sort of, I don't know, *strained* lately?

"But we all know why we're really here. [We don't, in fact.] We're here to honor a very *special* person. [No one has any idea who that might be.] I don't have to say who. A toast! To someone who *defines* specialness. Someone who will be in our hearts and minds, or anyway our hearts, forever!"

A few people raise their glasses uncertainly.

"And ever!"

One or two more.

"No, no, *not* me.

"Let me just say one thing. I hope none of you will let the fact that you all showed up in the same costume throw you off. These things happen. Last week at the enteritis gala, everyone came as either Ed Meese or Imelda Marcos. We looked around, we shared a few smiles, we proceeded to party hearty.

"Because isn't that America? What a country! Especially *lately*! Here's to good old-fashioned Yankee self-esteem!"

A number of people raise their glasses, not a few with feeling.

"I know we all have a lot of things to talk about, but I wonder whether, as we are all talking about them, we are all giving enough thought to those U.S.-inspired freedom fighters around the globe who are not just *talking* about squelching the Russian lust for a warm-water port—and may I remind you, Atlantic City is a warm-water port—but are *doing* it, with cold steel and hot lead.

"Do I see a few hangdog looks? Lose 'em! The *last* thing we're here for is to get down on ourselves. We know we would be over there right now, standing alongside these patriots—armed to the teeth, at home in the undergrowth, subsisting on snakes—if we didn't have obligations here.

"We all have . . . obligations. You know what I mean. To our obligations! May they never be silly ones, but our obligations whatever!"

With that you walk directly over to the hottest-looking member of the sex you favor, lower your voice *somewhat,* and say, "I see those eyes, you foxy rascal. Little eyes, little eyes, but big enough. Signals! If I can't pick up *signals,* at a *party,* like *this,* then where's style? Where's enchantment? Where's the social fabric?

"But I didn't come here to dally. Your thinking on the psycho-dollar! Float it, don't float it, what?"

But you are looking over his or her shoulder. "Jay!" you cry. There are bound to be three or four Jays. They blink. Pick the one who seems most satisfied to be a Jay, and exclaim,"Not *you,* Jay. I mean Jay-*o*!" Pick the one who seems least secure in his or her Jay-ness. "*There* you are," you cry. Move in on Jay. Kiss on the forehead.

"Uwe told me, 'Whatever you do, have a few giggles with Jay-o.' "

"Jay," says Jay defensively.

"I *think* it was Uwe. It can't have been *Nils,* can it? *Anyway,*" you say, "has Cerise got here yet, or do you know Cerise? Oh, if you don't know Cerise . . ."

Suddenly you start, like a deer in the forest. You are alert to something in the air, some tremor, some intimation, perhaps indeed some smell, that only you have the keenness to pick up on, so far. You raise your voice again, not quite to the volume at which you were making announcements but nearly.

"There is something," you say. "Something I can't quite put my finger on. There is a kind of . . . I *always* detect these things first. Sometimes I wish I weren't the one. But inevitably when I do, the thing grows, becomes . . . never mind. Let things take their course. I always say, a party wouldn't be a party without a certain . . ." You shrug.

(I am not saying this is how an Astor does it. You are not an Astor. An Astor has staff.)

And then you begin to undress, down to whatever layer of your ensemble most resembles tennis togs. You do this offhandedly, with the air of one who wants *others* to be comfortable. While you are doing it, in fact, you are circulating, and inquiring among your fellow guests as to who is up for singing.

"I don't believe we've met," you say to various ones in turn. "About time we gave some thought to what tunes we'll start launching into when we're a little more thoroughly oiled, *nicht wahr?* Know any good Civil War songs? How does it go? 'John Brown's body lies a-molderin' in the grave . . .' Or—any new verses to 'Waltz Me Around Again, Willie'? I don't know about you, but I have *had* sea chanteys. Doesn't it seem at every do lately it's chantey, chantey, chantey?"

Your hostess reaches your side. She seems about to suggest something. You speak first.

"This is rather awkward," you say, in a confidential but carrying tone. You look embarrassed, though by no means on your own account. "But, well . . . someone in here has lifted my watch."

While she is frisking the guests, that feeling comes over your sense of the Other—or maybe it *is* your sinuses—again. At a sign from you, concerned workers gather, bathing you in unguents and a fine, passage-clearing mist.

You have to accept.

SODOMY IN A FAMILY NEWSPAPER

*(Two Weeks as a Guest Columnist on
the* San Francisco Examiner)

. . . .

Breaking the Ice

Keep the cable cars. I have ridden them, and they work. They would make better time if fewer people stood on the sidewalk saying in small helpless voices to the gripman, "How do you get on?" But I am from near Atlanta and I live part-time in Mill River, Massachusetts, and part-time in New York City, and I have spent a fair amount of time in Waxahachie, Texas, and Los Angeles, and I can tell you that there aren't any cable cars in any of those places. Feel good about the cable cars.

And this Golden Gate Bridge. I believe it is the longest bridge in the world. Or in America. You'd better check me on that. Anyway, it is extremely long. And that's fine.

But I'll say this. Once, about fifteen years ago, I ran out of gas on the Golden Gate Bridge. And I got out of the car and wondered what to do. And I heard the voice of God:

"Get Back in Your Car."

I looked up and began to cry, thinking that providence had misread the situation, that someone up there figured I was fixing to jump, and cared. In a gruff sort of way. And I said, "Oh, no, don't worry. I'm just . . ."

"Get Back in Your Car."

"Please, sir," I snuffled. "It won't move."

"Get Back in Your Car."

So I got back in it and felt a slight jolt and heard, "Take It Out of Gear." And I realized that this was only the voice of the emergency vehicle that comes to push you across the Golden Gate Bridge when you run out of gas.

And that is how I lost my faith.

The truth is that for me, a simple Georgian, the Bay Area has often, over the years, been a source of disillusionment.

It was Pauline Kael, who comes from around here, who informed me when I mentioned *Gone with the Wind* that "it's *not . . . very . . . good.*"

"It's not?" I replied. It is the first movie I ever saw. I have seen it in each decade of my life. It is the story of Atlanta, the City Too Busy to Hate. The *good* Clark Gable urban disaster movie, I have sadly come to understand, is *San Francisco.*

It was this kid named Derek, who transferred to my grammar school from San Francisco, who told me that another pride of Atlanta was, well, malnutritional. Most kids in my school did not think there was anything so hot about being from San Francisco, but I knew that one of my heroes, Joe DiMaggio, was from there, and therefore San Francisco held as much glamour for me as Van Meter, Iowa. Which is where Bob Feller is from. So I listened when Derek told me that Coca-Cola was mostly sugar and water. I didn't see much wrong with that at the time, but Derek knew how to make ingredients sound despicable.

"What do they make where you're from?" I asked.

"Levi's," he said.

And what was I going to say? That Levi's were bad pants? Even in Georgia we knew better than that.

I grew up dreaming of being a four-sport immortal. That dream faded as my career expectations died—in some cases, as early as the fourth grade—in sport after sport. But I did manage to become a writer for *Sports Illustrated,* and I thought, well, at least I'll be able to hobnob with my childhood heroes.

It was Willie Mays, in Candlestick Park, who looked at me as if I were trying to sell him insurance. It was Joe DiMaggio, during his tenure as a coach of the Oakland A's, who looked at me as if I were wearing a garish yellow-and-green suit and white shoes, when in fact he was.

I grew up taking it for granted that I was a young person. And now I have a daughter who is twenty years old and studying to be a child psychologist. This would never have happened if she hadn't become a college student. We all know why children become child psychologists. Out of morbid fascination with what is wrong with their fathers. And do you know where my daughter Ennis got the idea to become twenty years old and take courses on the Paternal Fallacy? Stanford University.

In a couple of days, I will turn forty-five. (Instead of flowers, please send contributions to the Old Newsboy Fund.) That is not only old enough to be a twenty-year-old's father, it is old enough to be *my* father. And where will this happen? In San Francisco.

One other thing: When I got out of the Army, just about twenty years ago, I figured a person with such headlong youthful American gifts as mine should emulate Mark Twain, should heed Horace Greeley: should go West, should make his reputation in the city that was (I gathered from all the magazines) in full sixties flower as a *good* Babylon: San Francisco. I wrote the city's newspapers, enclosing samples of my writing. They said no thanks. I got a newspaper job in Atlanta. Saw first hand that my home city *could* find the time to hate.

And yet all these Bay Area–related shocks have not warped my natural objectivity and sweetness. I will be here as Writer in Residence for two weeks. On the whole I would rather be resident than write, but I have been vouchsafed a rare perspective on the City: a Russian Hill high-rise occupied by a disabused Georgian. (Me.) It is an angle I would be selfish not to share.

I will not come to you in tones of vengeance. In matters where you should feel every bit as secure as you want to, I will be supportive. The cable cars are fine. Do not, in this era of high tech, feel tempted to slick up the cable cars, to replace the clang with a contemporary electronic beep.

Do not, in this time of cutting back, give in to those who would have you shorten the Golden Gate Bridge. It is not too long.

Candlestick Park, now. Too much wind. If I had a chance to sit down with the city fathers—or whatever you call them locally—on the question of Candlestick Park, here is what I would advise, in essence: Less wind.

That's the way I see it. If I notice anyplace else where daylight needs to be shed over the next two weeks, I will speak out no less frankly. I come from Georgia, where we get down to cases. In my next column I will take up a matter which, in view of recent legal history, I feel obliged as a Georgian to clarify:

Sodomy.

Restaurants

"You'll get fat," people said when I arrived here. I scoffed. But sure enough, as I was walking up Russian Hill yesterday, I noticed my belt buckle was scraping the ground ever so slightly.

My, you have a lot of good restaurants here.

All right, I realize I said I was going to write about sodomy next.

I have been writing about sodomy next. But it isn't easy. There are all these loose ends. So to speak. That's one problem—every other sentence you have to say "so to speak."

Don't you worry, though. I'll deliver the sodomy column. And when I do, it will change the way you look at both sodomy and Georgia (where I come from) forever. One reason it hasn't been easy—writing about sodomy—is that you have so many good restaurants here.

And a lot of them serve alcohol, I notice. In fact, I've been meaning to ask someone—that place over on, I don't know, it's on a hill. Schlosch's. Is it possible that they get you to drinking there and pretend they've served you dinner?

"Are you ready for dessert, sir?" I remember the waiter asking.

"Oh, gosh, I don't know whether I could touch another . . . Wait a minute. Did I have my entree yet?"

He gave me an icy look, and what was I going to say? I'm from out of town. Next thing I knew (I was right in the middle of explaining why it isn't as easy as people think to write about sodomy) there was a plate in front of me with traces of raspberry purée and cheesecake on it.

"Will you be having an after-dinner drink, sir?"

I had seven.

I don't know about Schlosch's. But I think La Carte is great. That's where the description of the fare is so mouth-watering that you are served various dishes first, and if you can guess what they are (and "Fantasia of Various Fruits I Never Heard Of" isn't good enough), you get to read the menu.

Being a down-to-earth person at heart, I'm sure I'll return soon to Chowchow, where each customer gets a large yellow dog who lies at his or her feet and shares in the proceedings. My dog chanced to be an old newspaper dog, and was good company, at least until around one in the morning, when he started to howl.

If you prefer something lighter and more expensive, I would suggest Je M'Exquise, the Franco-Mexican haute cuisine spot that you have to drive over two bridges, or maybe the same bridge twice, to get to. I don't care how delicate or blistered your palate, the *huevos ranchereaux avec fines chilis calientes mousse* will melt on it. And don't miss the *cruditos*—essentially hearts of agave sprinkled with little shreds of money (no, not pesos, and not francs either—escudos, I think).

If you want something more basic—well, there's that Guatemalan place, what's the name of it? The truth is, I'm a little vague on some of these places. Eating well renders me kind of dreamy. But I do remember starting off with steamimg bowls of huello, which is basically white beans and red rice. Only there were little . . . what are those little things in huello, that look like . . . well, surely they're not what they look like.

Then there's Tapasissima, which specializes in the tiniest little tapas you are ever likely to see, if you can see them. Some are as small as a single bean. Though they aren't single beans, of course. They're beanskins stuffed with scallops and pork.

Snake 'n' Stuff is not for everybody, but I don't know where you'd find a better road-kill ragout—snake, armadillo, turtle, possum, owl. I forget just where this place is. Out on the highway. Decor runs to taxidermy.

Everybody loves hot dogs, especially hot dogs with personality. Bring the kids and grandparents alike to Furter Farm, which has clowns, long red balloons, and a dazzling array of hot-dog dishes: yard-longs, matzo-dogs, chopped frank salad, fried cross-sections, croissant-pups, fingerlings, hot and cold wurst soups, and various health dogs (bulgar is my favorite). After you top it all off with a great danish pastry or a big oblong dish of dalmatian ice cream, be sure to go out back for a leisurely tour of the wienery.

I haven't even mentioned Home, where if you go there they have to let you in; or Albanian Oasis, in the East Bay, where if you go there they throw you out; or Ferns Galore, where you let your salad drift down into your plate gradually from overhead; or the Erotic Steakhouse (the night I was there, though, the water bed was underheated and the gravy tended to congeal on my dinner partner); or any of the various Estonian (lots of eel), Italian, Chinese, or Italian-Chinese places (Emilio Fong for the best fortune gnocchi).

People keep asking me what I think about this latest Southern cuisine craze, Paul Don Prugh's Over-the-Sink. Every two customers get a faucet, which you drink out of; a sink, which you eat over; and a dish towel, for tidiness. Watermelon, unpeeled peaches, redi-mix tacos, buttermilk straight out of the half-gallon carton, and bacon-tomato-mayonnaise-mustard-pimiento cheese sandwiches on cheap white bread. I'll say this. I think Paul Don has slicked up his concept. Nobody I know who grew up on that food remembers there being any cilantro in the Sloppy Joes.

But, anyway. Sodomy. It's on its way. I told you it was on its way, didn't I? Maybe you're too young to remember the Carter administration. A Georgian never lies.

In fact that's probably why the restaurant over there in the Oakland section, the one started by that old boy from Georgia who used to work for Paul Don Prugh, looks like it's not going to make it. I tried to tell him. I said, if you want to start a sushi place, don't call it Bait.

In Another City, Dan Rather Is Pummeled, Asked, "Kenneth, What Is the Frequency?"

There's no getting around it. Dan Rather is a spy. When two well-dressed men accost someone on Park Avenue and pummel him and ask him, "Kenneth, what is the frequency?" over and over, he is a spy. That's all there is to it. Actually, that's not all there is to it.

The well-dressed men are spies. Kenneth is a spy.

I am a spy.

The story has been put out that I am here to write a sodomy column. Sodomy is my cover. The truth is that I am here about the frequency. Dan Rather knows perfectly well what the frequency is. So do I. So does the *Examiner,* but they've had a little trouble staying tuned to it, and I have perfect pitch.

That's how I'm able to do no real work (except write the George Will column and draw *Hi and Lois*) and still live in a lavish penthouse (Rather was on his way home from my place, where certain resources are kept) and breed rare tropical birds. I am paid $9,200 a day for my mastery of the frequency.

Of course we are all given preferential housing, long black (or, if we prefer, multicolored) automobiles and special hats almost like human hair that we wear to get on television. But I am the only one who every morning is delivered a fresh check for

$9,200 drawn on a Valparaiso bank and made out to Emory T. Hulme, or Fluhm, my real name. Some days I don't even cash it.

Everyone at the *Examiner* is a spy, except for certain key editors. The well-dressed men don't know the frequency. They are desperate to find out. So are a lot of people. That's why they bought NBC. Brokaw knows the frequency. Rather won it from him at racquetball. Jennings is not an American. The only foreigner who knows the frequency is Muammar al-Qaddafi. Sure. Give me a break. His real name is spelled Cuddehy.

Kenneth is the hairdresser. More important, he portrays LeRoy Neiman.

Armand Hammer does not exist. He, Wall Street, and the professional golf tour are imaginary.

Huey Lewis is a spy. He and Huey Newton are the same person.

We mess with your head.

It is a deadly serious game.

It all began with a few jaded college boys at Texas Christian University in 1957, but it is not a religious thing. It is bigger than that. It encompasses convenience store chains, Outward Bound, antihistamines, NOW, the America's Cup, what used to be the entire Big Ten, Post-it, Stephen King, cable, Wal-Mart, T-shirt empires, space, Joan Benoit, Brooks Brothers, the nation of Islam, and both Dakotas. That's where Brokaw fits in, he's from one of the Dakotas. If people only knew, NBC is incidental. We can take NBC or leave it alone.

It is hard to describe, in all its ramifications.

It could not exist without the frequency.

We made up the contras and Sandinistas, Whoopi Goldberg, abalone, the Kremlin, Kirlian auras, the Nielsen ratings (purely a device for publicizing the networks), subatomic particles, the State Department, and Merle Haggard. I know that's hard to believe (we've seen to that), but take it from me. Merle Haggard. (Isn't that what you'd name a country music legend if you made one up?) Oh, and shiatsu.

There were no women in the organization until Meryl Streep, last November. Now there are 107. Streep is 91 of them (including all the women on network TV). Before November, she was eight of the men. There are no women among the well-dressed men.

I might as well tell you our name: Myodos. It's Greek.

Basically we are a disinformation cartel. We control your reality. Every now and then Rather or Brokaw will interrupt his broadcast to don a Lone Ranger mask and say, in an odd high-pitched tone (not a clue), "Basically we are a disinformation cartel. We control your reality. I didn't say that."

And you say, "Oh." If anything. And then he tells you something has just happened in Peru.

Well-dressed men follow me all the time. I carry an Uzi. Rather thinks he can handle them with nothing but his dukes, but the well-dressed men (never the same ones) are getting bigger.

We don't know who the well-dressed men are. That's the only thing we don't know.

We don't care.

This infuriates them. They think we are afraid that they will get the frequency. This amuses us. Which infuriates them even more. Apparently they think Kenneth portrays Dan Rather. If you knew both men, you'd realize what a howl that is. Kenneth would never wear a sweater. You'd have to hold him down physically and put a sweater on him by force, and then he'd pull it right back off as soon as you let him up.

Kenneth sometimes changes the frequency. I am the first one he calls.

The well-dressed men are using high-power electron binoculars to read this as I write. You know what? They are not all that well-dressed.

They're swearing and cuffing each other now. They've disappeared behind something now. I can't believe how crude they are. You probably can, though. That's why we have a warm feeling for you. We need you. You believe things.

So do the well-dressed men.

And why am I telling you this? Am I finally so jaded that I'm blowing the whistle (not a clue) on all that has been built up over the years just for kicks?

I am telling you all this because the thing has turned ugly. A few hours ago I was taken out by certain key editors of the *Examiner*. They took me to a place called the M&M. (In other words, M's. In other words, Ms., which stands for manuscript. That's an inside joke. There are no manuscripts in the media today.) You know the expression "It only exists on paper"? It doesn't even exist on paper anymore. It is all on computers.) They took me to a place called Tosca. (An anagram for "Coast." Another inside joke. For the last two and a half years, approximately, there has been no actual land mass between the East and West coasts. We deleted it. We create the illusion of it by means of special videos in airplane windows.)

These editors asked me when I was going to turn in my sodomy column. I told them, in due time. But I could tell it was something else that was really bothering them.

Finally they came out with it. They didn't know the frequency. Everybody at the paper laughed at them because they weren't spies.

I looked in their eyes, saw the hurt there.

I thought back over the years. I was one of those original TCU boys. Our football team was the Horned Frogs (not a clue). Me and old Goat Bozer, Robert Bob Fligg, Garner Ted Armstrong, Nose Gullet, Bob Robert Pye, Aldyce Farmalee, and Kenneth. Oh, and Alger Hiss. Most of them are gone now. Kidnapped by the well-dressed men, grilled, accused of espionage, held for ransom.

We didn't care. The well-dressed men would telephone, say, "We've got Kenneth." We'd chuckle. A few days later: "We've got Kenneth now." Chuckle. "This time we *know* it's Kenneth." We're loving it.

And now it has come to this. Media guys, *Examiner* guys, our type of guys. Pouting.

I explained to them that the *Examiner* needed deniability. When someone accuses the paper of being nothing but a pack of spies, there had to be someone to say it wasn't true. Otherwise, no one would believe.

They said they knew all that, but they had a proposition for me. They exchanged glances. None of them wanted to be the first to speak. Finally, one did.

"We want to start a new thing," they said. "Call it Doomsy. Get our own frequency. Just us and you. You'd know how. And not tell the others."

I smiled sadly.

"No," I said.

"Why?" they asked.

"If you have to ask . . ." I said.

Then their expressions changed. Hardened. They were going ahead with it anyway, they said. If I didn't come in with them, I would see what would happen to me.

So it had come to this. What had started as a light-hearted jape had grown to magnificent proportions, had in effect changed the world—it had caused media people, *Examiner* people, to start acting like the well-dressed men.

I rose to leave. One key editor slipped noiselessly behind me, got down on his hands and knees. A second one pushed me. It was so obvious I went along with it. A third editor took a cigar cutter and severed the middle finger of my left hand.

Reeling with pain, I dashed back to the *Examiner*'s offices. And began to write.

The middle finger of my left hand hits the "e" key on the computer. They didn't think I could write without an "e."

They didn't reckon with my being an old hand at this game. Now that old Goat is gone, I'm the last person left in the media who can use a pencil. We can write with one hand.

They won't print this. Or they'll say I made it up. Or they

Why Not a National Sodomy Day?

Being from Georgia, I often feel obliged to explain something. At one time it was the Carter administration, and don't you wish it still were? Now it is sodomy. The law against sodomy that the U.S. Supreme Court refused to overturn this summer was a Georgia law. It *would* be, you're saying, which is easy for you to say.

This sodomy thing puts me in an awkward position. Say you were writing a sodomy song, rather than a love song;

> No doubt, a podomy
> Knew it was sodomy,
> But . . . here is the point of my song:
> Deep in the hodomy
> I knew it was sodomy
> But I just didn't think it was wrong.

You'd be defensive. Especially now that the U.S. Supreme Court is looking over your shoulder. The prudent course would be to deplore sodomy. Wash my hands of it. But I'm from Georgia. I feel accountable.

Michael Sragow, reviewing a Sigourney Weaver movie in the *Examiner* recently, noted that the movie doesn't indicate, as the book it is based on does, "that her paid sex is completely joyless, that she's constantly and sometimes painfully sodomized—or, as she puts it, 'bummed.' "

Nice to be writing in a paper where that point can be raised, as opposed to making a movie where it can't. But here's another point that needs raising: Sodomy is not always a bum trip. Not in Georgia, anyway. In Georgia it embraces forms of smooching which . . . Well, I'd be willing to bet—that all of these couples on these family sitcoms today—I don't want to name any names, but . . .

One reason sodomy thrives as a muddy concept is that breaking it down in specific detail is so hard in a family newspaper—even in this city, where the concept of family, I get the impression, is up in the air.

Hey, all concepts ought to be up in the air. Family will fly. Sodomy—the concept—should be shot down.

But first, I want to share with you the full measure of my expertise in this matter. In ruling that acts of homosexual sodomy in the home do not fall within the "zone of privacy" protected by the Constitution, the court rejected the argument that a 1969 decision, *Stanley* vs. *Georgia*, protected such acts. In *Stanley* vs. *Georgia* the court had reversed the conviction of a man for possession of "obscene matter" (stag films) in his own home. I am the man who—no, I am not that man. That was Stanley. I am the one who, in 1967, for the *Atlanta Journal*, covered Stanley's original trial.

Investigators rummaging through the man Stanley's drawers, in search of gambling materials, had instead discovered two flickery, somber, silent, dirty movies. The State Literature Commission (whose chairman observed under cross-examination that "we have nothing to do with great works of literature") had declared these films obscene, after showing them to selected Atlanta citizens. The defense put these arbiters of community standards on the stand, trying to prove that they didn't know obscenity from a hole in the ground. That attempt produced such exchanges as the following:

"Would you consider the picture of a nude woman without any clothes on obscene?"

"Yes."

"Have you ever been to the art museum, and seen the nude statues there?"

"No."

"Would you say that all art is nonobscene?"

"When it displays certain parts of the body it becomes obscene."

"What parts?"

"The lower parts."

"You've read all the works of Shakespeare?"

An optometrist: "Yes."

"You've read all the great works of literature?"

Same optometrist: "Yes."

Still the optometrist, warming to the subject of his qualifications: "I have seen painted art—I have seen some of the greatest art ever painted."

Then the defense attorney got to showing off, and asking citizens whether the *Decameron,* by Boccaccio, was obscene. Only he referred to it twice as "Decameron's *Boccaccio*" and once as "the works of Decameron of Boccaccio."

Later, in explaining these references, during a recess, to the court reporter, the attorney identified the work in question as *"The Canterbury Tales* by Boccaccio." When that failed to ring a bell, he said, "Don't you know the 'Old Wives' Tale,' by the miller's wife?"

He then went on, with something of a leer and unfortunately out of my hearing, to tell the tale—which, if it was as thorough a fusion of Boccaccio, Arnold Bennett, and two different Chaucerian tales as it promised to be, was a corker.

As for the films themselves, they were like sodomy in this sense: It was all in how you looked at them. As described in the indictment (". . . that said man did then take and place his . . ."), they lacked appeal. My ears did perk up when a testifying minister called them "sheer, pure and unadulterated filth," but that was for his choice of words.

The turnaround, to my way of thinking, came when the prosecution screened the films in court. Shades were improvised for the courtroom windows, the lights went out, and like magic the place was packed. Two-thirds of the people working in the courthouse must have left their desks.

An expectant hush. The first film, *Hot Blood,* began. An exhausted flabby man was shown lying on the floor next to a soiled bed occupied by two pallid trollops. Pallid, and yet somehow they moved in odd fresh ways. Something about the way their hair shifted. . . . Suddenly the man *tumbled up into* the bed. The screen went blank.

The film had not been rewound. We had been watching it backward. I was glad. That morose-looking man's strange ascension was one of the most eye-opening moments of my moviegoing life. Alley oop! Reversal. Obscene matter redeemed.

Not in the eyes of the Georgia court, though. Stanley was convicted. The Supreme Court reversed that decision, declaring that it was none of the government's business what people watched at home. (Would great things like that ever actually get declared, if it weren't for provocation from Georgia?) In those days (back when fewer of its members had been appointed by men from California), you could depend on the Supreme Court to check and balance Georgia.

Not anymore. In 1982 a man named (that's right) Hardwick was arrested for sodomy by a policeman who walked in on him while he was having oral sex with another man in his own bed. Hardwick was never prosecuted, but he sued to overturn the sodomy law. The wise old heads of the Supreme Court, citing the (that's right) "ancient roots" of aversion to homosexual sodomy, ruled against him.

I have a confession to make here. Watching two men cuddle, even, gives me the willies. But I figure that's my problem. I tried not to let it interfere with my appreciation of the movie *My Beautiful Laundrette,* which I thought was art; willies notwithstanding, it made my heart jump. The Supreme Court decision made it sink.

That decision was so much less sensible than a gay activist's reaction to it quoted in the *New York Times:* "Last year, the head of the Centers for Disease Control said that one of the best ways we can fight AIDS right now is to encourage stable, monogamous relationships among gay men. How can we encourage those relationships if we outlaw them and threaten to drive gay people underground?"

Sodomy and the family. The concept of the former drives gay men out of the latter. Some kind of reversal is needed.

Fortunately, Georgia's sodomy law has this crazy American virtue: It puts such a wide variety of people in the same boat that the boat won't float unless it's sounder than the concept of sodomy is. The concept of sodomy, explained in the right family newspaper, goes down.

In Georgia—and also in the District of Columbia, Maryland, Virginia, and sixteen other states where heterosexual as well as homosexual sodomy is outlawed—sodomy raises its head whenever anyone's genital factor comes into conjunction with anyone else's anal or oral. There is a nice lady doctor on radio and television who explicitly advises people *how* to sodomize. (At the last Giants home game, incidentally, I heard a fan shout at the umpire who ejected Vida Blue, "Your wife listens to Dr. Ruth!")

Unless I'm completely out of touch with American life, the pursuit of sodomy is such a common pluralistic institution, coast to coast, including Georgia, that anyone looking at our society from the outside would wonder why there is no National Consensual Sodomy Day. There can be few broader umbrellas, if that is the word, than sodomy, as defined by law. And yet it sounds nasty.

What we have here is a confusion of two things: the specter of sodomy and the practice of it. The specter is like the Drug Menace or Muammar al-Qaddafi, in providing an outlet for Americans' need to revile. (Specters corrupt.) The practice of sodomy is like public opinion, in that no given American is likely to be enthusiastic about the whole spectrum—but to say one band of the spectrum makes you or me blanch (small b) is not to say that there should be a law against its making my or your day. When the law proscribes just certain bands, it's discriminatory (which, currently, is okay with the Supreme Court). When it outlaws the whole spectrum, whom is it trying to kid?

We really ought to abandon the concept of sodomy. The only people it satisfies are those who get off on unreflective revulsion. Until recent years, when legislators have had to get more specific (and therefore have been overmatched by Dr. Ruth), sodomy was defined in every state's law books as "that heinous and abominable crime against nature not fit to be named among Christian people," or words to that effect.

Many people savor such language. But it leads to loose thinking. (One reason they savor it.) Justice Byron "Whizzer" White, speaking for the majority in the Supreme Court's close-the-door-on-sodomy decision, said "there is no such thing as a fundamental right to commit homosexual sodomy." (He reserved judgment on heterosexual sodomy, conceivably because someone nice was waiting for him in either Maryland, Virginia, or the District of Columbia.) That is begging the question. That is saying that the Founding Fathers did not feel protective against homosexual abominations.

I don't feel that way about homosexual abominations either. In fact I oppose them, on principle. But since I am from Georgia (and since the Supreme Court is acting as if it were running for office in Georgia in 1935), I am compelled to add what should go without saying: I abominate heterosexual abominations too. The Supreme Court would be a more effective deterrent to abominations if it gave more thought to what constitutes an abomination, and why.

BULLETIN: This just in. A local man, Frank Scarlett, Jr., who is originally from Georgia, has called to inform me that in St. Mary's, Georgia, a woman was recently arrested for performing sodomy in a nightclub, in the course of "some kind of bizarre contest they were having," according to Scarlett. Let me say that I am not in favor of competitive sodomy in nightclubs. But if it goes on in a town called St. Mary's, why name it after the city of Sodom?

Well, you'd feel silly arresting someone for "saintmarriage," or whatever the term would be. There's something about the ring of "sodomy" that's inimitably alienating. Even if you've never read the Bible.

In Genesis 19, it tells how a mob of Sodomites surrounded Lot's house, where he was entertaining some *angels,* for heaven's sake, and called on him to turn over those guys from out of town so they could sodomize them. Lot himself had been residing in Sodom only for a short time, like me. He didn't say, "For your information, 'those guys,' as you call them, are angels." Maybe he thought that would inflame the Sodomites more. Maybe he didn't want to sound like an out-of-towner.

What he did was, he offered the crowd his virgin daughters, to do with as they would. In what is probably the most insulting response in the scriptures, the crowd cried out, "No, we want those *guys.*" Whereupon the angels snatched Lot back inside the house and struck the Sodomites blind. Even in this state, the Sodomites kept trying to get at the angels, but after a while they got tired of trying to find the door to the house.

Later, after Lot had moved somewhere else and God had turned his wife into a pillar of salt, Lot's daughters got him drunk and slipped into bed with him, one by one, and got themselves pregnant by him. A bad business, all the way around, but a *heterogeneously* bad business.

A conscientious Georgian's position, at this point in history, is a variation on Lot's. The Supreme Court, crazed by lust, is standing outside the house hollering, "Give us those gays!" And the conscientious Georgian says, "How about some straight sodomites?" And the court cries, "No! We just want gays!"

And then—I don't know. It's confusing. I used to think the Supreme Court was in the role of the angels.

Warren Burger, who was still chief justice at the time of the sodomy decision and concurred in it, did not want to pass into the mists of history without making this observation: "Blackstone described 'the infamous crime against nature' as an offense of deeper malignity than rape, an heinous act 'the very mention of which is a disgrace to human nature.' " Well, I realize it isn't often nowadays that a person gets to say "an heinous," but you wouldn't think that even Warren Burger would happily cite an authority who thought consensual sodomy was worse than rape.

The only reason Blackstone or Burger or anyone else can get away with such a bizarre opinion is that the word "sodomy" sounds worse than the word "rape," which has an element of zing. The word for rape ought to be more repellent. So here's what we ought to do:

If we want to bandy the word "sodomy" around, we should redefine it, to mean rape, or sexual exploitation of a child, or reckless sexual endangerment, hetero or homo.

Then we could take all those willingly entered-upon acts that have heretofore been lumped together as sodomy, and give them a new civic name: denversion, miamy, minneapolism, winnetkatude, new yorkery (though people would ask, "What was wrong with the old yorkery?"), memphistry, atlanticity, dallasm, vegasation, bostoniousness, philadelphia, wheeling, berkeleylia, friscolity.

WHISKEY

. . . . .

The best whiskey I've tasted is Macallan Royal Wedding. It belongs to Greg Jaynes, but Patrick Lynch, who gave it to him, has agreed to keep it at his house because Greg, being from Memphis originally, would be liable to sit down some night and drink the whole bottle, which, except at the time, would be a shame.

Or maybe—this just occurred to me—the point is that Greg and I together would be liable to. I never drank a whole bottle of whiskey by myself—and now I never will because I have come to realize that even smaller portions can do me harm— but once in a Knoxville motel I did drink a fifth down to Lem Motlow's hat. Lem Motlow's picture, as I would not have to inform a cultured person, appears well down the side of a Jack Daniel's bottle. I had decided ahead of time that his hat was far enough, and oddly enough it was. So I didn't feel entirely unfunctional the next day, if it was the next day. And oddly enough it was.

Since then I have limited my horizons as to whiskey. It can be abused, is the thing, and without much effort. There is an old country song, "How Can Whiskey Only Six Years Old Whip a Man of Forty-three?" A blind blues singer in Mississippi threw up the half-pint of Wild Turkey with which I'd plied him. He'd said he needed "a little lift-up, to get my nerves started," but he hadn't been used to whiskey that good and had taken it too fast. Here's what his friend, another blues singer, remarked:

"Can't drink like a hog. I don't care who you with, you got to drink like folks."

I don't hang out with folks who would even consider drinking a whole fifth of whiskey, if it weren't as good as that Royal Wedding. It's a blend from Macallan's best barrel of 1948, birth year of Prince Charles, and of 1961, of Princess Di: two hearts in but a single malt. A paradox: So intensely scotch, it tasted somehow almost Irish. We sipped it and then we sipped some Black Bush, which is a higher form of Bushmill's (the notion, by the way, that some Irish whiskey is Catholic and some Protestant is an American canard): so intensely Irish it tasted somehow almost like scotch. You may think we were getting confused. No.

The Macallan, which is saying a great deal, was distinctly better. Richer. I never had any use for royalty before, but this whiskey had levels and then levels. We'd sit and sip it and stare off and think. Which is one reason it would be a shame to drink so much of it at once that you'd only have the impression you were thinking. My friend Gerald Duff once heard yet another blues singer stop in the middle of a song and holler, "It's hard for a drunk man to think," which is true enough; but sometimes it seems deceptively easy.

When I was a boy my mother told me that nobody liked the taste of strong drink. People just drank it to get tiddly. That was well known, she said. Given the nature of one-generation-to-another, I daresay there are some things I have misrepresented just as grossly to my children, but I never meant to. Which is not to say that my mother's point was entirely ill-founded. Liquor killed her father, after all.

We were a teetotaling Southern Methodist household. We lived in a dry county, but we'd have been dry if we'd lived in Gomorrah. My mother would do nearly anything for us, though, and once my sister Susan had to have beer for her hair. The girls in her class were using it, for luster. To get beer around Atlanta in those days you not only had to leave DeKalb County, you had to enter either a bar or a package store.

A bar was out. (How can it be that I, who still believe in Jesus' precepts, feel more at peace in a bar than a church?) And what if the preacher should drive past just as my mother was walking into a package store? Well, my mother figured that he would *know* she wasn't depraved enough to go into a package store for the purpose of obtaining liquor *to drink* (not that he wouldn't know it anyway, knowing her, but you never could tell), if she was seen going in there *with her fifteen-year-old son.*

So she made me go with her. I didn't want to—is putting it mildly. "We're just going to buy beer for my daughter's hair," she told everyone whose attention she could catch. "We don't drink, at all, in our house. We don't believe in it. We know nobody really likes the taste of it, they just drink it to get tiddly. This is my son. He's fifteen." This wasn't easy for my mother, who was shy with people she didn't know. And we weren't even in the package store yet. We were still out on the sidewalk. I think the reason Susan and I aren't dry, in our generation, is that we figured there was nothing we could do drunk ("You'll throw up on your pretty party dress" was one thing my mother told Susan) that could be as embarrassing as what my mother would do sober.

I can no longer swear to that. Once, at a wedding reception in Fort Worth, Texas, I did the limbo while carrying—I may have forgotten she was there—my sister-in-law Robin on my shoulders. Even without a rider, I don't limbo all that well. She banged the back of her head, and cried. She was only about fifteen. There's an old Irish song:

> *Whiskey, you're the devil,*
> *You're leading me astray,*
> *Over hills and mountains,*
> *And to Ameri-cay.*

Doesn't it taste good, though, and haven't I had some lovely times when it was served. I have drunk it with ballplayers, law officers, politicians, musicians, art critics. I'd have far fewer stories to tell today if I'd avoided it. Of course I'd remember even more of them if I'd had less of it.

I *like* gin. Much to be said for it. I like vodka. Beer's the thing on some occasions. But whiskey is more like food than white liquor is, and more essential than beer is. It has a roundness in the mouth, to be as spiky as it is. One reason I have to watch it is that I like it diluted only gradually, by ice. My friend Slick Lawson holds that you can't get a hangover if you stick resolutely to Jack Daniel's, because it's filtered through charcoal. My friend Dan Jenkins controls damage by having only J&B and water. To the English, whiskey means scotch, with water, no ice. I know it suggests a lack of character, but I fancy bourbon, scotch, Irish (the word "whiskey" is from the Gaelic *uisge beatha,* water of life), Canadian, Tennessee, and rye.

I know the history of writers and drink. Many of the friends with whom I used to partake most thirstily have quit altogether, because they got dependent on it, or it sapped their energies the next day, or their doctors warned them for the last time. One of them almost bled to death. It's a greater national health hazard than any other drug is. I don't drink in the daytime, and I feel a good deal younger during those hours if I've stayed away from it entirely for a while. Sometimes when I'm feeling run-down it doesn't even taste good to me, so I don't have any more (after trying another swallow to make sure). Taking everything (so far) into consideration, I still like it. "The only time I ever felt very close to my father," a woman friend of mine says, "was in the church just before my wedding. We had some whiskey."

In New Delhi every Sunday, thousands of devotees bring bottles of Indian whiskey, with names like Double Dog, Drum Beater, and Black Bird, to the temple of Bhairon, a Hindu deity. His image is black-skinned, it has a sinister mustache, and it holds in its four hands a demon's severed head, a bowl, a bottle of whiskey, and a club. Temple workers pour the worshipers' whiskey into the idol's gaping mouth and it dribbles down into a tray below, which seems a shame.

"In Hinduism," says a religious scholar named Dr. Lokesh Chandra, "the divine and the satanic are not distinguished. Individuals have an element of both. If your child is very ill, you might go to Bhairon and say, 'You have the experience of all the terrible calamities, so take me out of mine.' Bhairon is the ferocious aspect of the divine. He is pleased only with things that are not normal—human blood, whiskey, and so on.'"

There's a country song in that.

> *Human blood,*
> *Whiskey and so on—*
> *That's about all*
> *I got to go on.*

The worst whiskey I ever tasted was at four o'clock in the morning on the front porch of a man in Florida who was reputed to have a wonderful coon dog. I've forgotten now what the dog's great distinction was said to be, but *Sports Illustrated* had suggested I look into it.

We were out in the woods for six hours with the dog and the man's son, who was about fifteen. "He's a real old hunter, ain't you, Forrest?" the man said. Forrest didn't want to go. More interested in girls these days, the man said. Forrest wouldn't even talk to us, and his father had to keep nagging him, trying to get him to show some interest. Forrest would make disrespectful noises under his breath.

It was muddy and overcast. The dog led us into nearly unnegotiable brushy lowlands. And just as the man was saying, "I wouldn't feed a dog that ran trash," which was to say a dog that pursued anything other than racoons, his dog led us through briers to a hollow log that turned out to have a possum in it. Then the dog was off on the scent of something which, when treed after a long scrabbling sloshy chase, turned out to be a house cat. You'd have to have been around coonhunters to know how bad that was. Forrest went off home by himself.

The father and the dog and I went back, too. We sat on the front porch looking at the morning mist. I told him I would come back some other night when the weather and the moon were better, but we both knew I wouldn't. I had never had a night when my own stock had sunk quite that low, in front of key witnesses, but I knew I probably would. The man brought out an old syrup bottle with a cork in it.

"No tax stamp on this," the man said. It wasn't the proverbial white lightning; from what I was able to see it was dark yellowish. It was harsh enough, Lord knows. Yet it tasted semisweetly of corn, among who knew what other things. And there was something kind of oily about it.

It was pretty good.

THE LIQUEFACTION
OF YOUR HOME

I hear from American Express regularly, but this letter was special. It urged me to "acquire funds quickly and easily" by taking out a line of credit against the equity of my home. "Why is the American Express Equity Resource Line right for you?" the letter asked. "Because now your home can give back some of the good things you've put into it."

It had never occurred to me until then that my home owed me money.

In some ways I even feel beholden to my home. My home is larger than I am, it preceded me, it is built to last longer. I always know where to find it. My home is substantive enough to fall back on, were I truly hard pressed; but were I truly hard pressed, American Express would not be offering me money. (I live mostly in the country. Not significantly agricultural country, but I have seen all those movies. I know what kind of trouble folks like you and me and Jessica Lange got into after lenders flooded their family farms with credit. American Express's desire to invest in my home gives me a dream: I am trying to pick my juicy garden tomatoes but can't, because my arms are pinioned by what should be life preservers but are instead thousands of dollars' worth of heavily financed and defaulted-upon tractor tires.) My home keeps me and my household warm and dry, cool and lubricated.

But not necessarily on my terms. Any given sequence of clicks, gurgles, whoofs, and silences may signify that my home's plumbing and heating system is operating the way it is supposed to or that it is getting ready to dissolve the very concepts of *operation, way,* and *supposed.* One moment I am sitting all toasty in my domain, and the next moment hot water is seeping through the walls.

Someone, a student of economics or of plumbing, I forget which, told me once that aspiring economists study plumbing: the way pipes work is somehow a model of the way money flows. That equation is just fathomable to me, because plumbing and economics alike aren't. My home's plumbing and heating involve untold variables, from OPEC to sweated nipples to mice. To be an intellectually honest student of my home's plumbing and heating is to be as out of one's depth, projectionwise, as a perfectly candid economist. Since, I conclude from long experience, no one can live or plumb in absolute radical uncertainty, there are no intellectually honest students of my home's plumbing and heating.

I don't mean to complain. Doubtless a principle of equity applies—homes begin to resemble the people they house. I might be at a loss with predictable, sound-as-a-yen plumbing. And my plumbing today is a day at the beach compared with what I was immersed in years ago when I rented a mobile home. The bathroom was so small that I had to take a shower stooped over. One morning I got the hot water turned up too high, lost my bearings trying to adjust the knobs, and couldn't escape until finally I burst scalded out into the living-dining area, wearing much of the shower apparatus. Another morning I awoke beside a steamy freshet. The water heater had exceeded itself in the night and caused something to burst, and I was looking from my bed into a rushing stream that traversed not only the mobile home but, I found after wading outside, the whole trailer court. It is amazing to see what a little plumbing can do. I watched the stream that sprang from my residence steadily lengthen, way on out toward the horizon. When I called my landlord, he came over and sighed.

"Every time I try to own something," he said, "it just wants to back up on me. I don't know; Misty and I lived here before we . . . the truth is, she went off with the Culligan man. I see now I didn't do a lot of the *little* things. Not realizing. But, hell, she looked down into the sink all the time. I asked her why and she wouldn't say and she wouldn't say and finally she said if I had just once in six months ever thanked her for being her. So, hell, I started to then, but she stopped me. She said she didn't feel like she was her anymore. I don't know why I hold on to this place." Tears welled up in his eyes. American Express does not confront all that may happen when homes start giving back what people put into them.

For nearly a century my home was a parsonage. When we tore out an exterior wall we found a surprisingly lurid lining of tracts and Sunday-school lessons, which spoke, not cozily, of final things: poor girls frozen in the snow, rich men too preoccupied to be washed in the blood. When relieved of that wall and its literature, my home brightened. My home knows how to have a good time. Still, there is a heritage there, one that I would be loath to place in the hands of any more money changers than necessary.

If I were to follow American Express's advice and take a brisk creditor's stance toward my home, I know I would pay for it. Have you heard Tammy Wynette and her daughter Tina render a song called "No Charge"? Little Tina pipes up, asking to be renumerated for chores. Then Tammy weighs in: "For the nine months I carried you, growing inside me: No charge." Would you like to hear that sung to you all night by plumbing?

Granted, mine is not an eighties home. I bought it two digits ago, for just five digits down and a handily single-digit mortgage. That was before Money got hotter than Peace and Love and became the most absorbing thing in America.

Today, I realize, the sort of deal proposed by American Express is making a big splash. More and more Americans are borrowing on what is sunk into their homes to get the cash it takes to float the kind of life-styles that people who live in the kinds of homes they live in have been led to expect. According to *The New York Times,* "Americans have just begun to dent the equity in their homes built up over years of rising real estate prices. Some $4.3 trillion of unmortgaged equity still remains to be tapped as collateral." "Tapped," is it? That attitude toward shelter is over my head.

The headline on that *Times* story, let it be noted, was PUTTING THE HOMESTEAD DEEPER INTO HOCK. A *Newsweek* piece on this trend was headlined SQUEEZING YOUR HOUSE FOR CASH. Headlines, because they fall back on idiom, have their own barometrics.

Unless you can talk your home into making the *payments* on one of these loans, I think it is hazardous to treat your domicile as a deep pocket. To reside, to be sure, is to be at sea. But if my home and I are going to take a plunge, we are going to take one that has dash and moral implications, and one in which my home's distinctive properties are enlisted. For example—well, if this were in fact what I contemplated doing, exactly, I wouldn't be talking about it. But picture the following headline and subheads:

ROGUE HOME, OWNER PLUNDER AMEX VAULT

GUARDS BAFFLED BY JETS
OF HOT AND COLD WATER

Freebooter Steams Off
in Converted Parsonage

THE UNBEARABLE LIGHTNESS OF AIR TRAVEL

. . . . .

Okay. You are somewhere, at least in theory, between Butte and Mobile, going faster than sound in a long metal container that is not in physical contact with anything. A slight jiggling sensation at your prostate (if you have one) is, essentially, all that is holding you up 30,000 feet above something that looks like a badly distressed suede jacket but is in fact the surface of the earth. You have been served a brown puddle with a lump in it, a rectangle of pale-yellow congealment, and some kind of mineral-based salad. There is a *wheeeeengneeeenngn* noise. The jiggle-at-the-prostate feeling gives way to a kind of giving-way sensation. You are swallowed by a cloud.

Rule One: Maintain perspective. You don't *know* what it's like to travel from Butte to Mobile by camel. Especially these days. If camel travel has gone as far downhill as air travel, it may not be appreciably more salubrious than flying.

I will say this, though. In a moment I am going to give you the other seven rules for staying physically and mentally sound while hurtling through the air in a fifth-rate diner, but first I want to say this:

If man had been meant to fly, he would not have been given the Eastern shuttle.

I single out the Eastern shuttle only because no other service has ever flown me from Boston's Logan Airport to Boston's Logan Airport in six hours.

On November 13, 1986, I boarded the 7 P.M. Eastern shuttle, whose stated purpose is to transport people from Boston to New York. I was, I thought, at the end of a book-promotion tour. The fog of publicity had permeated every fiber of my self-concept. My blood was two thirds radio-station coffee. My sinuses felt just on the verge of giving birth to alien beings larger—certainly *thicker*—than myself. I had set foot in an average of 1.78 airports per day over the preceding three weeks. But soon I would be in a bed I could call my own. I thought.

Logan to New York's La Guardia is supposed to take thirty-five minutes. We sat on the ground for two hours. We took off and headed south and then circled La Guardia for a while. Then we landed in Providence, Rhode Island, and sat on the ground there—too far from the terminal for disembarking—for a couple of hours. From time to time our pilot offered us a terse explanation:

"There is only one runway open in La Guardia, and that one has a crane on it."

"New York has turned to worms."

"We don't like this any better than you do."

We flew back to Boston. There, at 1 A.M., we were free to sit in the airport until 7 A.M., when we would have an opportunity to try the shuttle again. Or else we could go out into the rain and find ourselves a hotel room (nearest available ones were in Cambridge) at our expense. There were some two hundred of us. If we wanted our tickets back, we had to wait for a single agent to read out each passenger's name in a soft, disconsolate, unamplified voice: "Farquarharson . . . Farquarharson . . ." Sigh. "Van Wilderwiesel? . . . Van Wilder . . . *mie*sel? . . ." Sigh.

My point is that you, the passenger, cannot count on the airlines to keep air travel from running you into the ground. You must follow the Eight Rules of Self-Preservation. Here are the other seven:

Two: Remember that flight stress may cause the human body to implode. The best way to prevent this is to put the considerable likelihood of it out of your mind. If you have already used a nasal spray and yet you can feel the clog in your sinuses growing denser and more expansive, try not to think about it. Thinking about it causes brain matter to merge with the clog to form a lavalike compound that is even more dangerous to think about than the clog alone. Your entire shoulder-and-upper-back area may be drawn up into your Eustachian tubes. If this happens, try not to think about it. In any event, don't resort to the nasal spray again. If you're going to become addicted to something, it might as well be something more glamorous, like glue.

Three: Don't listen to anything airline personnel tell you. Particularly "We don't like this any better than you do." Fury only heightens flight symptoms. *No one knows* what is meant by "There is only one runway open, and that one has a crane on it."

Four: Don't make eye contact with other people's children. Other people's children in flight are not like small human beings as we know them on earth. They are more like indefatigably flopping, vividly inedible-looking rough fish that are too large to be in the boat with you and too profoundly entangled in your gear to be thrown back. If one tiny speck of glop from an airline meal gets on the elbow of a belted-down flying child, that glop will inevitably be transferred onto every surface and down into every crevice within a radius of six to seven feet. Children in aisles are like shadowy figures in dark alleys.

Five: Do not accept any food from an airline that you would not accept from a vendor in Calcutta. If it's bottled or if you peel it yourself, it may be all right. Otherwise it may stay with you for the rest of your life.

Six: Breathe a lot before you board. The air on airplanes (air air) is not oxygen but $D_2PE_3FG_4UN_x$: two parts dread, one plastic, three exhalant, four frustrated gravity, and an unknown amount of unknown. Make every effort to keep it away from your lungs.

Seven: When traveling by air, try not to bring anything with you. If you check it, it falls into the hands of people who may send it to Puerto Rico (unless you are going to Puerto Rico), or may subject it to certain pressures that make it look like New York Mayor Ed Koch's body, or may play the Carousel Game with it.

Here, briefly, is how the Carousel Game is played. Handlers unload baggage from the plane to a holding area, where they sit on the luggage and peer through tiny peepholes at the crowds forming in the baggage-claim area. The players try to match up—mentally—various bags with people waiting. Then they place bets. Then they break for lunch. When they return one will say, "Wanna toss something on the carousel?" Discussions follow. What the handlers want to avoid is for the first bags on the carousel to be those belonging to the persons who have jostled their way closest to the carousel. The game proceeds at its own pace.

If you try to carry items on, then you run into problems. Airplanes themselves have developed intense sinus congestion. If there were room for a comfortable majority of passengers to carry items on and tuck them away, the Carousel Game would suffer and the airlines would have union problems. So today's leaner, meaner aircraft has fewer closets; overhead compartments are half filled with luggage from last month; and, in many cases, flights are canceled so that they may be combined with other flights to produce cabin areas that are tight as ticks. If, an hour or so after scheduled lift-off, some interstices remain uncrammed, then airline employees' relatives, dressed in two or three overcoats each and carrying prostheses to be inserted into pockets of leg room, are hastily summoned and wedged in. (Unavoidably, this may occasion slight delays, since some of these relatives live a couple of hours from the airport.)

Eight: Don't let yourself be frustrated. Frustration is bad for the traveler's system. Frustration *is* the airlines' system. When you set out on an aerial voyage, always have a *realistic goal* in mind. Tell yourself firmly and briskly, "Well, if I actually spend some time in the air headed in the right direction during the next twenty-four hours, I'll consider it a day well spent." As you take off from Butte on the first leg of your passage to Mobile, relax. Sit back in your seat, think how much more nearly fitted to the human body this seat is than a camel, and reflect: "By golly, it won't be long now before I find myself magically transported to Mobile. Or Butte. Or someplace that may well lie in between."

Unseen Rock City

O h, yeah, they're real rubies all right," I heard the man saying at the end of the bar. "Visitors are asked not to take more than a handful apiece, but say a little kid fills up a paper sack with them, I look the other way."

Some loony, I figured. The guy he was talking to must have had the same reaction: He said something noncommittal, put a ten on the bar, and muttered, "See ya."

"See Rock City," the man who'd been talking about rubies replied, in a friendly, earnest tone.

I have never seen Rock City. All my life I have been seeing the "See Rock City" signs, and I have always assumed that someday I would get around to seeing the city itself, and Ruby Falls and seven states from atop Lookout Mountain. In Sunday school when I heard about Satan taking Jesus up on the mountaintop and showing him the world, I thought of Rock City. Only I never thought of it in any kind of infernal light. On the contrary. Good to know it was up there.

"You've seen Rock City?" I called down the bar.

The man's eyes lit on me. He didn't look crazy; just affable.

"Seen it?" he said. "I run it." He moved to the stool nearest me. I don't usually care for forwardness in bars, but he seemed okay.

"So who's minding the store?"

"Oh, it doesn't take much minding. There are always plenty of the regulars around, they know how things operate. And in case somebody new stops by while I'm gone, I leave a note by the door, saying, "Come on in, enjoy yourself."

"Wait a minute. You're the whole staff?"

"Staff? You could say that." He smiled.

"Well, what do you mean, 'in case somebody new stops by'? There must be thousands of new visitors every day."

His face fell a bit. "Well, that's what people assume. But it's just not true, I'm afraid. Every so often someone drops in, but—"

"I can't believe that," I said. "All those signs! All those people seeing them!"

"Mm," he said. "You've never seen Rock City, have you?"

"Well, no. How'd you know?"

"I'd've remembered you. And when was the last time you talked to anyone who had seen Rock City?"

"Well . . ."

He sighed. "And think what they're missing. I was just telling that fellow, the one who had to leave, about Ruby Falls."

"I *thought* that's what you were talking about. You don't mean to tell me—"

"And the view from Lookout is something to behold."

"Can you really see seven states?"

"Sure. And what people don't realize is, one of them's Maine and another one's Montana."

"*What?*"

"Sure. When it's really clear you can make out the top of Coit Tower in San Francisco, but we don't even count that. We only count states whose *land* you can see. We don't count foreign countries, either."

"Now wait a minute."

"And you know—people think 'Rock' just has to do with stones. It has to do with music, too."

"Oh yeah? You've got live bands?"

He smiled. "We've got some of the best."

"Like who?"

"Oh, Elvis, and—"

"Elvis at Rock City?"

"Uh-huh. You can't beat the acoustics in those natural caverns, and then, too, you know Elvis. He likes throwing rubies at Montana."

"Likes?" I said with a smile.

"Well, *loves* is more like it."

"No, I mean: love-*duh,* don't you mean?" I chuckled.

"Oh," he said. "Mm."

"You know what?" I told him. "Maybe your problem is your signs. Maybe you ought to try something more modern. 'Welcome to Rock City Time,' or 'Rock City Is It!' "

"Maybe," he said. "I don't know, though. Sometimes I think, hey, if people don't want to see seven states it's their own lookout."

"Yeah, but: 'See Rock City.' On the one hand, you kind of take it for granted. On the other hand, it's pretty stark. It might even put people off. Like all those 'Prepare to Meet Thy God' signs."

"Well," he said, "of course those are mine, too."

HOW TO WALK IN NEW YORK

I grew up in the South. I can do the traipse, I can do the gallivant, I can do the lollygag, and I can do the slow lope. I can hotfoot it, I can waltz right in and waltz right out, or I can just be poking or dragging or plowing along. As a youngster I skedaddled. I believe that if called upon, for the sake of some all-in-good-fun theatrical, I could sashay. But I know that these gaits have their places, and on the other hand there is New York walking.

You think you know how to walk in New York? No you don't, unless you *know* you know how to walk in New York. Otherwise you just impede the flow.

You have to walk with vigilance, looking unconcerned. You have to walk like you have an angle. Knowing where you're going but aware of what's around, ready to deal with weirdness but your feet on the ground. You have to walk like a serious person. Or such a crazy person that everybody gives you a wide berth, which is also serious.

Serious. Not stately. In New York stately walking doesn't work—it's not urban.

"You ain't country enough to get over a Decatur County fence," said an old south Georgia pol to an Atlanta reporter who got his pants leg caught on some bob wire while interviewing the pol as they walked across some fields. To be a New York walker (sometimes called Nyok wokkuh), you have to be *big city* enough to cut through three nuns, two dogs being intimate against their walkers' wills, a four-vehicle fender-bender, and a multilingual fistfight without missing a beat or making *any* kind of contact with *any*body and then to take an intersection of Broadway and a major cross street in stride—diagonally against both lights— while someone is coming from the other direction pursued by transit police and a bus is trying to turn left in your face.

You can't intimidate a bus. You can't fake a bus. But you can time your cut around the bus in such a way that you're using the bus as interference. Against most cabs, you can stick pretty much to your route, because as a cabdriver once told me, "I hate hitting pedestrians. You got to fill out all these forms, and you got to dot every *i* and cross every *t*." But you can't be bluffing. You've got to be clearly prepared to take the hit. And to be fair you've got to give the cab a way to avoid you without losing momentum. If you don't do that, the whole system breaks down. New York walking is like broken-field running, only it's a whole field of running backs all trying to *just barely* avoid being stopped without actually running.

I can walk in New York. One day before last Christmas I *shopped* 4.36265 miles.

The truth is you don't measure New York walking in miles. You measure it in blocks. Four uptown-downtown blocks in three minutes is a pretty good pace. The reason I took a mileage reading is that I was trying to see how walking-boom gear and techniques can be equipped to New York walking.

I bought a pedometer at Urban Hiker, a store on Amsterdam Avenue that is capitalizing on the walking boom. I didn't get a pedometer that gives you time of day, elapsed time, and heart rate because I didn't want to wire myself up and then be punching a lot of buttons. Just a basic Monitor brand Free Style pedometer with my average stride programmed into it—which, right there, is already departing from New York walking principles, because how do you know how many short strides, side steps, stutter steps, jukes, and glides you're going to take?

I also bought walking shoes, walking socks, walking hat, walking sweat suit, walking jacket, walking gloves, and walking pack. I didn't get a walking stick or an ultrasonic hand-held dog repeller because in New York you don't have room to use a stick and the dogs aren't trying to stop anybody from walking—they're walking too.

We have a walking boom in America today because we have to have a boom in something. And people have come to realize that running jars the joints. Walking is the exercise trend. Which means you need high-performance socks. The Rockport Walking Sock produces "a unique pumping action that aids circulation, forcing oxygenated blood out of the walker's foot and back up into the calf so legs and feet won't tire and cramp." The "padded, bulb toe allows toes to spread naturally during walking motion," while the "padded heel cup absorbs shock of heel strike, holds sock firmly in place."

And Wigwam's new Trek sock has "outstanding wicking characteristics." If you don't have polypropylene in your socks, to wick foot perspiration away from your feet, then your socks aren't in on the boom. By the same token, my Helly-Hanson LIFA polypropylene hat wicks away head sweat, and although I guess there is no poly-anything in my 100 percent cotton Naturalife sweat suit and jacket by Daniel Cleary, I have the impression that they wick too, though maybe I am wrong there.

I tend to pronate. I learned that from the salesman at Urban Hiker while trying on shoes. Pronating means turning your ankles in. That doesn't mean I need a special pronater's shoe. It just means I was sold shoes by someone who wasn't afraid to get into biomechanics.

My shoe for fitness is the black New Balance with EVA polyurethane sole. Polyurethane doesn't wick; it is light and long-wearing. I can describe my New Balances in layman's terms: nice and comfortable. For technical reasons I also bought the Donner Mountain shoe, which the man in the store described as "fast-forward casual," and which has EVA high-performance polyurethane sole, mudguard, saddle, dip for Achilles tendon, full leather lining, and cantilever heel. The Donner Mountain is regarded as relatively dressy, even though it's red. And ugly. But how could I pass up a cantilever heel—surely the last word in features, I thought—until I saw an ad in *The Walking Magazine* for L.A. Gear's Workout Walker, which has a "medial wing for added support and stability," a "spring rocket profile to provide natural walking motion," a "midsole full C.M.E. 4 durometer wedge to interact with each individual foot function," "promenading plugs," "tractable flex bars," and "360-degree reflective material for night visibility."

But I wouldn't buy anything called L. A. Gear for New York walking. Furthermore, I don't want to walk around with the sinking feeling that I am not so highly developed an organism as my shoes are. I'd be inclined to rebel against shoes designed that *insistently* for walking. Feel like doing something else in them, just to show who's boss. I remember the first time my friend Jim Seay tried on a pair of garish modern solid-state plastic ski boots. He leaned one way and they held him up. He leaned another way and they held him up. "These would be some good drinking shoes," he said.

You see people walking well in New York in all kinds of shoes, including too-small old wing tips slit at the sides for comfort. Frankly, I don't find that I walk any better now that I am outfitted.

Nor do I feel the need for walking lessons. The New York Walkers Club holds a power-walking clinic every Saturday at 9 A.M. at the Ninetieth Street and Fifth Avenue entrance of Central Park—or so I was informed. Out of curiosity, I showed up. Twice. Saturday, December 19, and Saturday, January 3. I was there. Where were *you*, clinic? Teach *me* to walk in New York!

Each time I showed up at 8:55 and waited until 9:03. Already embarrassing myself as a New York walker by staying in one place for eight minutes. And then I ankled. All untrained and unsupervised amid joggers, walkers, cyclists—not my crowd.

And on the second Saturday I beheld a vision. Was *passed* by a vision. A woman who must have been six foot three, walking next to a man nearly as tall who was jogging to keep up with her. She had tense blond hair barely contained by a sweatband, she was "split high," as football scouts say about prospects with extremely long legs, and she was flat-out walking.

My mother walked fast. My sister walks fast. My kids walk fast. I have never been seriously involved with a woman who didn't walk fast. I humped my hips, pumped my arms, and rose to this woman's challenge.

And she got smaller and smaller. She wasn't making exaggerated movements; she was just a fine-tuned walking machine. Finally I had to sprint to catch up with her.

"Excuse me," I puffed. "You are some walker."

She nodded, still just a-chugging. She and her companion both eyed me narrowly. "I can't run," she said. "Bad knees."

"Where'd you learn to walk like that?" I asked.

"There's a clinic . . ." she said.

"It seems to have knocked off for the holidays," I said. "So how can this be power walking? Power never knocks off."

She shrugged. It seemed to throw her rhythm off slightly and she bore down harder and I was tired of running and she started getting smaller and smaller again.

Okay. But tell me this. Can you power-walk in the street? Not if shrugging interferes with it. New York walking involves shrugging, yelling, dodging, sidling, ducking, occasional carefully considered contributions to the homeless, and—here's the big thing—looking and listening.

New York walking isn't exercise: it's a continually showing make-your-own movie. Hit the street anytime and it's always going on. Young mother leading a little kid, he pulls back and starts crying and she keeps right on, she's going to leave him there, go to the park by herself, she's had enough—*who will win this battle of wills?* And an old lady querying a bemused toddler, "Sugar, did you drop that great big cookie?" as she's undoing a baggie to come up with another great big cookie—and on the other hand here's a grandmother telling a pouting kid, "You *have* to learn to *memorize*."

And two guys in fur hats:

"So what's new, Abe?"

"Ah. The same goddam thing. Nothing."

And here is a man wearing two buttons with italics: "Reagan *Knew*" and "How *dare* you assume I'm a heterosexual."

Every kind of hat. Every kind of eyes. A man with *psst* tattooed on his arm.

And whatever I'm wearing, however I'm moving, I am a camera in walking gear.

BUDDY, CAN YOU SPARE
A SOCIAL POLICY?

. . . .

I guess there is no practice so bizarre but some tribe can be found that practices it. Somebody was telling me the other day about some culture somewhere—Indians, I think—in which the whole issue of poverty is finessed. If a villager can't work, for whatever reason, everybody chips in to keep him or her reasonably prosperous. And this policy is cheerfully applied even if the person in question just doesn't *want* to work. Most people in this culture, apparently, have a proclivity for gainful employment. If some people don't, what's the use of outrage or consternation?

That village, wherever it is, is less complex than New York. Every day, and more and more pressingly in this era of fast-and-loose conservatism, people in New York who have spare change are confronted by fellow pedestrians who claim, and in most cases appear, to be in desperate need of it. At a time when the most influential person in the land is Nancy Reagan, many citizens do not feel safe in assuming that these mendicants are just being perverse. Therefore, the unneedy feel a need to formulate some coherent and (not an eighties term, but) "compassionate" policy toward beggardom.

"I only give money to old men," says my friend Joanna. "Young people can earn it and old women yell at you if you don't give it to them."

"I give it to old women," says my friend Esther. "Because it's *so sad*. . . . Unless they're dressed better than I am. There's one on the corner of Bergdorf's who's got a different outfit on every day! Who is *she* kidding?"

"The ones that smell like pee," says my friend Julie. "Because I figure no one's going to hire them."

"Or if they're too fat, or too ugly, or schizophrenic," says my friend Elaine. "If they're too out of it to be employed. But I never give anything to the regulars in my neighborhood. Otherwise, every time I went out the door they'd be saying, 'Hey Elaine, gimme a dollar, quick, I got to get uptown.' "

My friend Roland picks up a sandwich when he goes to lunch and hands it to a genuinely wretched-looking man who stands near his office. The man appreciates it. But Esther says she offered a sandwich to a man who was holding up a sign that said HUNGRY and he told her he only accepted money.

"I give them something if I'm happy," says my friend Nancy, "or if I'm feeling the weight of the world, or if I'm feeling morally majestic. . . ."

The panhandler with the least appealing approach I have heard of was the one who went up to two women and, when one said, "No, I just barely have enough to get home," responded as follows: "Now, wait a minute. There's two of you. That'll cost you on the subway two bucks between you. What are you going to do, take a *cab*? Even that couldn't be more than. . . . *Hey!* Okay, go home and sit in your *kitchen,* and have your big meal in your *kitchen.* I ain't got no *kitchen.* You old stingy lesbos!"

The best approach is to be a young pregnant woman, looking worried and shy but determined, with a wisp of hair in your face.

I don't know why nearly all of the people I've quoted are women. It may be that women think over their responses to panhandlers more thoroughly because, as several of them pointed out to me, a woman has to stop and open up her purse and dig around in it as potential snatchers look on.

My own giving has tended to be casual and impulsive. If the

beggar isn't surly, and I have some loose change in my pocket and I am not feeling surly myself, I hand him or her a couple of coins, checking quickly to make sure none of them are tokens. Surely a greater percentage of my charitable dollar reaches the deserving that way than if I attend a concert or send a check to an agency.

I now realize that the matter warrants more consideration.

I am one of those villagers who do have a natural tendency to work. I would do it if I didn't have to. And I get to make money doing something I get off on. Once, when I was employed by *Sports Illustrated* and was doing a story on coon hunting, a coon hunter in Spanish Fort, Texas, told me something I was tired of hearing—that I had the greatest job in the world. I said, well, I had to spend a lot of time in airports and one thing and another. He said, "I bet it beats running three saws eight hours a day." He worked in a sawmill. I admitted he was right.

That man might have contended that begging beats journalism, even, but there he would have been wrong. I feel qualified to say so, because my work—buttonholing people, trying to get something out of them, holding their attention, choosing words, telling my story, making a case—is not much different from what panhandlers do, and my working conditions and remuneration are better. The same things could be said about panhandling vis-à-vis a lot of work in New York: sales, law, entertainment, advertising.

Panhandlers are as much a part of the New York culture as investment bankers, certainly, and it is not clear to me that they are more of a drag on it. Their readily observable proliferation in the era of country-club self-reliance bolsters my politics. Edwin Meese may be right in asserting that some people just want to be homeless, but why does Reaganomics seem to *bring out* this longing in people? Outspoken traditional Democrats have not exactly been a dime a dozen over the last few years; the chance to talk to one is well worth a quarter.

Generally speaking, people who try to bum money off me in

person have less of it than I do. This is not true of a great many other persons and institutions that try to hustle me. Just by floating depositor's checks—refusing to let them withdraw their money until five, ten working days after they deposit it—banks grift more brazenly than beggars.

Dealing with New York beggars at their work is generally less stressful than dealing with, say, New York bank tellers at theirs. Beggars are glad to see you. Some of them are obnoxious—I can't say I *blame* them—but most seem to recognize that it behooves them to deal agreeably with the public.

My policy toward them is twofold.

One: to regard panhandling as critically as I do any other profession. There are beggars who persuade me and beggars who don't. The former get my business. I have the feeling I can discriminate between beggars more surely than I can between doctors, for instance. Which is a shame, because I can go a lot further wrong with the wrong doctor.

Two: to converse more with selected beggars. The other night I talked, or listened, to Carol for half an hour across the street from her welfare hotel. She said she lives in one room with her mother and nineteen-year-old son, who has bad kidney trouble and partial brain damage and won't go to the doctor anymore because the last time he went, the doctor told him he was going to die; and if he doesn't go to the doctor and get forms signed, they can't get all the benefits they're entitled to. She said she was distantly related to Fanny Brice, and here she was out on the street asking for money!

"Last night a man gave me a dollar, and the woman with him said, 'She'll just spend it on liquor.' I caught up with them and gave it back. I said, 'I don't drink and don't smoke and don't use drugs and I'm not a hooker.' This woman goes into the deli and comes back and says she's glad I took the trouble to tell her that. She gives me ten dollars."

People kept walking by and I told Carol not to ignore potential donors for the sake of talking to me. "I like talking," she said, and she went into more detail about the family connection with Fanny Brice. "It is distant," she admitted. "But. . . ."

Panhandlers shouldn't be taken for granted. The other day, I saw a woman sitting on a hydrant, holding out a cardboard coffee cup. She was the least complacent-looking person I'd seen in some time. Her mouth was set in a grimace that would have been fitting if she'd just heard that a loved one she'd been feuding with had died. She was looking off into the distance. I went over and extended a handful of change toward her cup. She pulled it back. "No, thank you," she said firmly. "I *have* some change." Her cup was half full of black coffee.

Another time, I was walking down upper Broadway with a box of fried chicken in my hand, eating out of it greasily. A guy came up to me with his palm out. I pulled the last piece of chicken from the box and offered it, greasily, to him.

"Naw, naw," he said.

"You don't want it?" I asked him.

"Naw."

"How come?"

His expression showed that the moment had become awkward for him. "I don't *know* you," he said.

Don't walk on the unknown warrior

I am no pageantry buff. One crowd of geezers in solemn assembly with hats on that no sober kindergartner would wear with confidence is all the same as another to me, and I will never be king of anything because I can't sit through coronations. Another thing I can't see is sights. Museums are so often full of museum pieces. Cathedrals don't need me. Let monuments work their side of the street and I will work mine. I am more interested in, for instance, rare old conjunctions. I saw one on my last trip to London, on a hotel-lobby sign advising passersby that the Gentlemen's Toilet was closed for repairs.

WE REGRET ANY DISCOMFORT OCCASIONED, the sign said, WHILST THIS SCHEME OF IMPROVEMENT IS IN PROGRESS.

But every so often a student of travel has to brush up on certain other basics. For instance, I had not seen a Woman Who Thought Everything Was Bigger (or Smaller) Than She Thought It Was in some time. Hence, a bus tour. "Discovering London," said the brochure. "A unique day of history, pageantry, sights, and entertrainment."

I told some English people I was going to see the Crown Jewels and all.

"How odd," said one.

"The only person I've known who went to see the Crown Jewels," said another, "was arrested for trying to steal them."

First stop, the Albert Hall. I guess it was the Albert Hall. If I have any doubts, it is because our tour leader said it was the Albert Hall, and she was the one who referred to "Dr. Johnson, the lexographer, and Samuel Boswell" and told us we were having authentic fish-and-chips when we were having bad french fries and heavily encrusted patties of something that *might* have been vaguely, formerly, aquatic. What I would go for is a serious, informed fish-and-chips tour. I've always wanted to improve my sense of plaice.

I will say this: Our tour had an excellent Man Who Had Seen All This Before. An Ohioan in London on a church-related convention, he was squiring the wives of two of his fellow conveners. His not having any pressing sessions to attend all day had the potential to desex him, as you can imagine, and he compensated with knowingness. When One of the Wives asked him what he thought she could say to cause a bearskin-hatted Queen's Guard to change his expression, The Man Who Had Seen All This Before said, "They've heard it all."

"What if you said something about the Queen?" asked The Other Wife.

"I doubt sincerely you could say anything," he said, "that these men haven't heard."

But I am getting ahead of the tour. On the bus at the Albert Hall, we groupers huddled tentatively. "Am I in the right place?" said the Woman Who Looked Agitated.

"Yes, indeed," said our guide. The woman looked even more agitated. That was the last we saw of her.

Our guide was a wiry schoolteacher. Her eyes really lit up three times:

—When she spoke of leading a group of children at a brisk pace up the steps to the top of the dome of St. Paul's. "It is lovely," she said, "standing next to a nine-year-old who is panting and you're not."

—When she introduced us to the swarthiest birds I have ever seen, the ravens of the Tower of London, who were gathered around a block where, over the centuries, a number of people have been beheaded. They were waiting for tidbits, she said.

—When she recommended that we take in the London Dungeon, a museum of torture, on our own. "You will see nasty scenes," she said. "You will see prisoners in the Tower, for instance, being eaten by rats. We often bring our schoolchildren here to learn what was done by the rulers of England."

"Oh, goo'ness," said the Woman Who Said "Oh, Goo'ness."

"How much do you want for it?" asked the Man Who Guessed the English Just Can't Imagine Living the Way We Do. He also asked that about St. Paul's and Buckingham Palace. Our guide had, after all, informed us that Egyptian millionaires had bought Harrods and a rich American had bought the London Bridge.

Three of us were Japanese and silent. One was German and kept going to sleep. One was from St. Kitts and was always the one who was missing but turned up. The other twenty-some-odd of us seemed to be American.

Two other things that, quite aside from whether or not they were true, we learned:

—In 1908 a woman of traditional leanings broke up a meeting of suffragettes in the Albert Hall by lowering herself into one of the enormous organ pipes, waiting patiently until the suffragettes assembled the next day, and then making terrible noises in there. It took two days to get her out.

—The Soho area of London got its name from the hunting cry of an illegitimate son of Charles II and Nell Gwyn. He used to hunt in that area. Crying, "Soho, soho!"

"You should begin to feel already a good few vibrations here," our guide said from the front of the bus.

"What is she talking about?" said the Man Who Had Actually Bought a Plastic Bobby's Helmet.

"Brompton Oratory, I heard her say," said the Man Too Large to Share a Seat.

"Ah, uh-huh," said the Man Who Had Seen All This Before.

"Underneath," said our guide (presumably about something else), "you were neatly skewered."

As to pageantry, we heard more about it than we actually saw. Is the Queen's Garden Party pageantry? I suppose it is. Our guide told us about it. You used to get four sandwiches, now two, she said. In Westminster Abbey, we saw in person the altar where we had seen a queen crowned and princesses married on TV, but there wasn't anything going on there at the moment except for several other groups looking at it with us. One of us thought it looked a *lot* bigger than she had thought.

"Why can't we walk on the Unknown Warrior?" asked the Teenager Who Would Never Take Another Trip with Her Parents.

"Patsy, please," said Her Mother.

"Well, we walked on Edward the Sixth and Dickens."

"I don't believe that was *them*. I believe that was just plaques."

"It *was* them. And Ben Jonson she said was buried standing up. So we walked on his *head.*"

"Patsy, now . . ." said Her Father.

We didn't view the time-honored and stirring ceremony of the Changing of the Guard. We did see the Guard.

"I thought we were going to see it change," said The Man Too Large to Share a Seat.

"Only on alternative days," said our guide.

"And this isn't an alternative day?" said the Man Who Was Trying to Get Over Something Back Home.

"That'd've been yesterday," said the Man Who Had Seen All This Before. "And tomorrow."

Many of us took a number of photographs from the Westminster Bridge. "I'd like to get the Houses of Parliament when the sun is on it," said the Man Who Had Seen All This Before.

"I guess that's on alternative days," said the Teenager.

"What would you rather live in, a new house or an old house?" asked the Man Who Guessed the English Just Can't Imagine

Living the Way We Do, after he had offered to buy the Sword of Spiritual Justice, the Sword of Mercy, the Rod of Equity, and various orbs, scepters, and crowns, as beefeaters reminded us to keep moving past the Crown Jewels."

"Oh, I rather like my mod cons," said our guide. "But if I could have a thirteenth-century cottage with—"

"What's mod cons?" he asked.

"Running water. Hot. And—"

"You wouldn't rather have something new with a Jacuzzi?" He nudged the Teenager, who wouldn't make eye contact.

"No," said our guide.

Lunch was at the Cockney Cabaret and Music Hall on Charing Cross Road. I've told you about the fish-and-chips. Entertainment was a pianist playing "Strangers in the Night," "The Sound of Music," "That Old Black Magic," and other favorites. One of the waiters, as he served us, sang along with "Strangers in the Night" in Her Father's ear.

"Are you an actor?" Her Father asked accusingly.

"Sweet of you," said the waiter.

Our guide and the Man Too Large to Share a Seat danced, briefly and indeterminately, to the "Beer Barrel Polka."

The Man Who Was Trying to Get Over Something Back Home said he was a druggist. He had been held up five times. (That's not what he was trying to get over.) "Guns in your face, it's an experience," he said. Demerol, morphine, and anything with codeine in it. Each time, at 11 A.M. "I don't know what it is about eleven in the morning," he said.

He and I slipped away from the rest of the group while they were going through St. Paul's. We had pints of Guinness and the *Evening News,* whose big story of the day was MAN BITES OFF BOUNCER'S NIPPLE.

"We ought to show this to our guide," he said. "But, I don't know . . ." He told me a little bit about what he was getting over, and then he drifted back over the holdups.

I asked him what gunmen tended to say to him.

"Oh, you know, something to the effect that they're counting on me. Not to move, I guess. Two of them said—it's funny, you know what two different ones of them said? 'This is the real thing.'"

NO SENSE LENDING MY BODY AN EAR

. . . .

Listen to your body."

That's what healthfolk tell you. Supposedly, your body knows.
If you ought to stop doing something, your body will tell you. If
you shouldn't do it in the first place, your body will tell you. If
you ought to start doing it, your body will tell you.

Right.

A couple of years ago, I went through a period of intense
health consciousness—purism as to diet and fidelity as to
exercise—and my body said things like "You don't really want
that ice cream." Which I knew to be a lie. And "What are we just
sitting here for? Let's get up and leap and thrust and fling and
strain until our heart is pounding!" Which made my work—the
squeezing of quite enough but not too many words in between
carefully selected marks of punctuation—impracticable.

So I subsided into temperance. A middle course between
wholesomeness and degeneracy. And now my body is its old
self: a Tower of Babel. Living in my body is like driving a station
wagon full of three-to-twelve-year-old children. I can't tune my
body out entirely, and if I try to tune in all its voices distinctly
enough to figure out what they are carrying on about, I can't
keep my eyes on the road.

Speaking of eyes, my left one at this moment is saying, "Uh,
I believe there's something, maybe not, maybe it's jusss . . ."

"Just what?"

"Jussst . . . one of those feelings. That an eye gets sometimes. As if there's something—maybe a speck of dust, maybe the seed of some horrible growth—just over here to the left of the tear duct, and . . ."

Meanwhile, my neck-and-between-the-shoulders area is going: "Ooo. Ung. Ohhhh. Mnk. Uhhh . . ."

"*Yes?*" I reply.

"Oh, uh. Didn't mean to interrupt."

"Well, then don't. I'm just beginning to perceive the connection between the rise of fundamentalism and the proliferation of subatomic particles, and—"

"Connection. Yeah," says the neck-and-between-the-shoulders-area. "Somewhere there's a connection not right, because, ooo, ngk, ummng . . ."

"Would you at least speak English?"

"Well, it's kinda hard to put into words . . . uh . . . twinge . . . uh . . . dull, kinda, ache. . . . Couldya roll your head kinda—oh—no, ow! That's . . . crackle . . . nngg . . ."

How much of that can a person listen to? Not that my body does nothing but gripe. Sometimes it screams. This morning I put my right foot into this big moon-boot house slipper I have a pair of, and all of a sudden the place between my third and fourth toes—a precinct I seldom hear from—exclaimed:

"WHOA! TROUBLE! ALERT! SOMETHING AWFUL!"

"What? How could it be something awful?" my mind put in.

"Sure! Right! That's easy for a mind to say," cried my intertoe gap. "A mind has no feeling! I'm telling you, THIS IS HORRIBLE! YOWTCH!"

So I pulled my foot out. There was pain. No denying that. But a person's feet sometimes have little cramps here and there. I didn't examine the affected spot carefully. It was too early in the morning.

"OH! MERCY! DON'T PUT ME BACK IN THERE! GET HELP!" cried the place between my toes.

I turned my slipper boot over and shook it. A wasp wobbled out.

"See! See!" cried my entire foot. "Look at that thing! I *knew* it was awful. Wasp! Wasp! I'M GOING TO START SWELLING SO ALL YOUR TOES WILL BE PRESSED SO PAINFULLY AGAINST THE SIDES OF YOUR SHOE YOU WON'T BE ABLE TO WALK, YOU WON'T BE ABLE TO GET ANY WORK DONE, I'LL BE YELLING AND HOLLERING AND——"

"Cool it," my mind told me and my foot at the same time. Meaning, to me, put some ice on it, and, to my foot, put a sock on it.

And my mind was right. My feet—perhaps because I stepped on so many bees as a barefoot child that my soles got weary of rendering themselves convex—handle insect stings very well. So why don't my feet, themselves, remember that? If I didn't take what my body says with a grain of salt, I would run around like—there is no other phrase for it—a chicken with its head cut off.

And we have been talking just about pain, so far. We haven't even touched on pleasure. Pleasure is worse.

My body and I both like pleasure. That's the problem. For instance, my body *loves* to taste. Also to swallow, to get a little buzz on, and to lie around digesting.

I was standing in the kitchen last evening, about six o'clock, and my tastebuds were clamoring, "Spaghetti! Spaghetti! With a whole lot of homemade sauce with hamburger and mushrooms and peppers and onions and Parmesan cheese! Come on! Can we? Pleeeeze?"

And my mind was saying, "Wellll . . ."

And my stomach was saying, "I'm not so sure."

And my going-to-the-trouble-of-cooking muscles were saying, "Nahhh . . ."

And my conscience was saying, "Raw carrots! Raw carrots!"

And all of a sudden several parts of my body, in one voice, said, "How about a nice glass of bourbon with some ice in it?"

"No," I said. "We're not going to drink. We've got too much work to do."

"Well, hey," my body said (more and more voices chiming in), "you know we want you to get that work done. 'Cause we feel good when you do. Well, sometimes. But we almost *always* feel good when we have a nice glass of—"

"No," I said. "You know what the mind and I resolved yesterday. Nothing to drink, at all, till we get this work done."

"Hm," said my body. "Sounds kind of *abstract*. Sounds kind of *dogmatic*. Thought you were a tolerant, open-minded, visceral kind of fella. And what was it you were saying the other night? 'The body is the measure of all things'?"

"You heard that, did you?"

"I've got ears."

"Ears, yes. Sense, no."

"Sense!" cried my body. "I've got five senses. And a glass of bourbon would look good, taste good, and smell good, and the ice would make a nice little clinking sound. And it would make me feel good."

"While you were drinking it. But then you'd want more. And then tomorrow morning—remember last Sunday morning? Remember what you were saying then?"

"Well, vaguely, but . . . well, no."

Fortunately my mind jumped in. "Okay, that's it," it said. "End of discussion. We'll go ahead and make spaghetti, but no bourbon."

"Oh yeah?" said my body.

"Yeah," I said.

"You are *no fun*!" said my body. "I'm getting a headache." And it pouted. My body pouts!

So. I guess you think you know what my conclusion is going to be. That what I should do is listen to my mind.

No. I don't think so. For one thing, my mind is usually far less opinionated than my body. It is inclined to say, "Oh, well, all right. It's your body."

For another thing—let's consider exercise. My body enjoys physical activity. It feels better after working out. But try to tell it that. The weather is beautiful and someone wants me to go bike riding and what does my body say?

It says, "Uhhhhh. Nahhh. Mmf. Not now. Feeling kind of heavy right now. Kind of like not really doing anything drastic, you know? Feeling pretty tied up right now with this dull ache around the shoulder blades, and the sentiment on the part of the legs here is just sort of . . . blah."

And what is my mind saying. The trouble is, this suits my mind just fine. My mind is saying, "Well, actually I was thinking it might be better to sit around taking stock this afternoon. Kind of light stock-taking. There are so many things to sort of halfway worry about, you know."

My mind doesn't have a great deal to say to my body, directly. The truth is that I have translated most of the body language in this essay from the original drone, with every now and then a yelp, a plea. Nor is my body at all self-conscious about this. It feels that its level of expression is more basic than anything my mind can understand. Whereas my mind finds most of what my body says to be such an old, subrational story that my mind drifts away, and there I am, alone with sluggish animal sounds—which, however, are almost preferable to the vague, staticky signals my mind is sending back from wherever it has drifted to. Usually my mind and my body ignore each other and nag at me.

But I can't count on that. You know what happened this morning? Before the wasp? First let me say that I resolved last night to arise bright and early and get to work. Very important. I put both mind and body on notice that we were going to jump right out of bed.

Okay. This morning. Seven o'clock. The alarm went off. And here's what my body said:

"Ooohhh. Feeeels sooo gooood in here. Just gettin' com-mmf'table. Ummm. Lessss jussss dooozzze back offff."

And do you know what my mind said? I know this is strange, but it actually happened. My mind, just completely out of the blue, and with none of its too-frequent archness, said:

"Hey! I know what! We can just watch this movie here, which is about er, um, something you need to know for your work. Sure! That's a good idea!"

This movie? What movie? There was no movie—no *screen*—anywhere in sight. Even if there had been, my eyes weren't open.

But I fell for it. I went back to sleep. *Dreaming that I was watching an educational film.*

And do you know why I did it?

Because my body said, "Listen to your mind."

II. OIL AND WATER

EXERCISE BOOKS AREN'T AEROBIC

xercise books and I never seem to work out. It is not in my nature to read anything for ulterior purposes, except maps, and sometimes even there I eschew routedness to frolic in the names of rivers. Sure, I read with an agenda: to become a better person. But in hard-to-specify respects.

That much is *my* problem. But exercise books, for their part, also have something to account for: why they never approach literature.

Can you imagine Ralph Waldo Emerson writing an exercise book?

"Hence, instead of Man Exercising, we have the exercisist, who values the sit-up as such. That man is seated; more sedentary than he knows. I had better never know of a workout than to be enthralled by its representation in a Work of Exercise."

Emily Dickinson?

> She reckoned Flesh a Hinge—
> Then tensile as a Seed
> In Compost roistering—
> Sprung outward, and was dead.

Edgar Allan Poe?

"At such times, though I longed to loosen the fiendishly binding fibers of my frame, yet did I refrain, held back—let me confess, though the reader regard me with loathing—by an absolute *dread* of the stretch."

T.S. Eliot?

> *Unreal Body*
> *Stoop stoop stoop stoop*
> *Ugh ugh ugh ugh*
> *Between the bend*
> *And the reach*
> *Between the squat*
> *And the thrust*
> *Between the gasp*
> *And the surge*
> Balompbomp
> *Falls the Roll of Fat.*

Flannery O'Connor?

"The no-armed man was doing his lift-ups the first time he saw Elbalene Verge come looming up the baked clay road. She was jogging, larger and larger, and larger yet, till she stopped and there she stood. 'Mercy in this world,' she said when she got her breath. 'If you ain't purely something. You ever had a faith kinesiologist pop your neck?' "

Robert Lowell?

> *My whole face is sunset red.*
> *My willed motor is running hot.*
> *Poor legs! I am tired.*
> *My Uncle Devereux died of rot.*

E.E. Cummings?

> *if huff and puff lift off of* oof
> *that May be canned by dint of wont*

> —*far* *were* *up* ...
> *limber bob and down*
> *heroic in the Hellespont*

In fact, these authors would no doubt have written more positively about exercise, if they had put their cadences to it. Or they would now, in this age of (impropriety and) fitness: I am jaundiced, from having read a pile of actual, contemporary books that deal with exercise. The idea was that I would be moved to try out what they prescribe. Gardening writers make you want to garden, food writers to eat, fishing writers to angle. *Must* exercise writers make you want to go to bed with a good book?

If you ask me, *Gary Yanker's Sportswalking,* by Gary Yanker (Contemporary Books; paper, $8.95), runs walking (not to mention Gary Yanker) into the ground. "For a time," Mr. Yanker writes, "the broad base of walkers were content to remain anonymous and practice their sport in a personal, unorganized way." No longer, apparently. Certainly not since 1983, when "walking reached a turning point with the first exercise book, *The Complete Book of Exercise-walking* [by Gary Yanker], and its successor, *Gary Yanker's Walking Workouts.*"

My two favorite passages in *Gary Yanker's Sportswalking,* by Gary Yanker, are these:

• *"Safety*—Walking is not only the safest exercise, it is probably also the safest sport with the fewest injuries. The two biggest problems are blisters and falling down. The one is not serious, and the other occurs in many sports and can be minimized with care and concentration."

• "Striding began in 1984."

Apparently, running is out these days and walking is in. *Going the Distance: The Right Way to Exercise for People Over Forty,* by Ronald M. Lawrence and Sandra Rosenzweig (Jeremy P. Tarcher/St. Martin's, $15.95), a straightforward and cheerful but not effusive book that I found readable but ungalvanizing,

says that two of the many ailments running can cause are "painful bleeding under toenails" and "excruciating pain in the ball of the foot." We are also told:
- "Making love is strenuous but not aerobic."
- "If you want to know whether you're working at a nice, moderate aerobic level, ask yourself: am I smiling? If you are, you can't possibly be working too hard."

If you ask yourself whether you are smiling and the answer is a ringing "Yes!" then I doubt very seriously that you are reading *Walk, Don't Die: How to Stay Fit, Trim and Healthy Without Killing Yourself,* by Fred A. Stutman (Medical Manor Books; cloth, $18.95; paper, $9.95). Here is an example of the verse that Dr. Stutman has a tendency to break into:

> *Now if you need another reason*
> *Why you should walk each season*
> *You should know that sitting too often*
> *Will put you in an early coffin*
> *So, remember, Walk, Don't Die*
> *If you want to stay alive*

The brothers Busen, who are pictured throughout *Tae Kwon Do for Beginners: A Karate Program of Fitness and Self-Defense,* by Werner and Franz Busen with Robert Hofler, and with photographs by Klaus Laubmayer (Fireside/Simon & Schuster, paper, $10.95), say: "We came to tae kwon do for purely superficial reasons: We wanted to look great." In the face, they both look like Max Headroom. Their bodies look like Max Headroom's must. Or, if you prefer, like Max Muscleroom. Sometimes they are shown squaring off against each other. In the section on self-defense, one of them is shown squaring off against a young woman, who gives him his comeuppance. I am glad.

The Busens are never smiling. They look as if they are under enormous, well, to borrow a phrase from Charles Atlas, *dynamic tension.* If a person has already made the decision to take up tae kwon do, then this book would doubtless be helpful. In me, this book immediately stirred a feeling of *déjà whew.*

The people in the illustrations of the forthcoming *Greater Energy at Your Fingertips: How to Easily Increase Your Vitality in Ten Minutes,* by Michael Reed Gach (Celestial Arts, paper, $8.95), look far more comfortable. I decided to get in touch with my Sea of Energy.

The Sea of Energy is just below the navel. What you do, according to Mr. Gach, is as follows:

1. Place one of your fists over the point between your pubic bone and your navel.
2. Place the palm of your hand over your fist.
3. Gently lie down on your stomach with your hands in this position.

Okay, now, everybody. Try gently lying down on your stomach while holding your hands in the pit of it. I fell on my face, knocked my reading glasses awry, and lay there stunned and wondering how, with or without glasses, I could be expected to read Step 4 in that position.

A spirit of marketing is alive in many exercise books. *Feeling Fit in Your 40s,* by Richard Benyo and Rhonda Provost (Atheneum, $14.95), is addressed quite explicitly to Baby Boomers, who, it seems, are now engaged explosively in entering their forties. I can't wait until they all turn ninety. "Look at your fortieth birthday," the authors suggest, "as a board from which to dive into the refreshing pool of opportunity: in health, fitness, professions, lifestyle." Having passed that birthday handily, I look at it as a board with which to whack any writer who addresses me, or anyone else, as a "Boomer."

Remar Sutton's Body Worry, by Remar Sutton (Viking, $17.95), is an account of, yes, Remar Sutton's year-long transformation of himself from a bulbous wienie to, in his own eyes, a hunk. It made me want to transfer myself into Irving Howe, who gets a different class of book to review. "Now, intellectually," Mr. Sutton writes, "I know the shape of my body isn't important. I am happy my life has been guided more by the meatiness of the mind than the shallowness of muscle tissues. . . . But I'm still very capable of a trite and shallow thought or two." But self-knowledge goes only so far.

I am glad to have on hand, for future reference, *Peak Condition: Winning Strategies to Prevent, Treat, and Rehabilitate Sports Injuries,* by James G. Garrick and Peter Radetsky (Crown, $17.95). If you are already painfully into exercise, this book will tell you how to prevent, treat, and rehabilitate sports injuries. If you should develop a ganglion, or fluid-filled cyst, on the back of your wrist, you may be comforted to know that "the traditional treatment involves the family Bible. Not prayer, that is, but smashing the Bible onto your wrist and breaking the ganglion." That's what I call demystified sports medicine. Furthermore, the authors say, "the thing to do with jammed fingers is leave them alone."

I have concluded, with some regret, that that is also what I will do henceforth with *Deep Bodywork and Personal Development: Harmonizing Our Bodies, Emotions, and Thoughts,* by Jack W. Painter (Bodymind Books, 450 Hillside Ave., Mill Valley, Calif, 94941; $19 including postage). A couple of the extraordinary self-manipulatory exercises prescribed by Mr. Painter made me feel better, but I am wary, for legal reasons, of this one:

"Have a partner surprise you by screaming or shouting at you several times without giving notice. React as fully as you can."

From the introduction to *Deep Bodywork* (by Ron Kurtz, the author of *The Body Reveals*):

"Jack's book involves both mind and body, and he sees them as one. He sees this more truly than anyone before him. Let me quote: 'Rather than viewing the body, the bodymind, as a many layered onion, I see it as a vibrant plastic mass, less viscous in some places than others, and composed of the same interflowing stuff from outside to inside and inside to outside. Thus when touched at any level or depth, it instantaneously responds, re-shaping itself in every other dimension and part.' Now that's wholism."

And so is this: pedaling for half an hour on a good stationary bicycle, which leaves your hands and eyes free to take your mind off exercise, as such, by reading Walt Whitman.

COKE PEPSIFIED

. . . .

The most noted invention of the eighties, surely, is new Coke. But certain questions remain.

Must "market points" dictate formula?

The Coca-Cola Company, although it still holds a lion's share of soft-drink sales, has seen that share shrink by several market points. Each of those points represents $250 million in sales. Therefore Coke has come up with a taste that is flatter, sweeter—more like that of its leading competitor, Pepsi. By that logic, if *60 Minutes* started losing ratings points to *Fame*, Mike Wallace would start break-dancing. The Reagan administration has done something similar in Latin America: in order to stop the spread of Marxism-Leninism, it has adopted a stance that smacks of the Brezhnev Doctrine. Someone should look into the feasibility of assigning precise economic value to what we might call "integrity points."

Is it idle to speak of soft drinks and imperialism in the same breath?

The spread of Coke bottles into far-off climes has long been a symbol of—some would say—pushy Americanization. There has never been an ickier expression of we-are-the-worldism than the well-known Coke jingle:

I'd like to teach the world to sing
In perfect harmony.
I'd like to buy [sic] the world a Coke
And keep it company.

If a freedom-loving person were forced to choose between a world in which all people waved Coke bottles and one in which all people waved hammers and sickles, he would presumably take the former. But he wouldn't love it. Especially if Coke is going to change as the wind blows. What if China makes a soft drink that tastes like fermented rice and Coke loses more market points?

Setting aside international implications for a moment, is what we are seeing here the Repepsipublicanizing of America?

For years Pepsi was the GOP pop, Coke the Democratic. Donald M. Kendall, the chairman of the board and chief executive officer of Pepsico, Inc., is a longtime friend of President Richard Nixon's, and during the Nixon administration, Pepsi entered Russia. Jimmy Carter, while readying his presidential campaign, called the Coca-Cola Company "my own state department," and during the Carter administration, Coke entered China. Then Reagan took upon himself the mantles of FDR, JFK, and Truman; Pepsi signed up Geraldine Ferraro; and Coke became more like Pepsi. What is left of Coke, or of the Democratic Party, as we have known it?

Isn't changing the name of non-Pepsified Coke to Classic Coke a bit much?

A bit much, yes, but very eighties: i.e., shameless. Noncolorized film classics may soon be marketed as Classic Classics.

And how about this writer's personal reactions?

Until the change, I had always thought of Coke as, relatively speaking, the class act. This belief might be ascribed to my having grown up right outside Atlanta, Coke's corporate and ancestral home. But I was exposed from an early age to Coke and Pepsi both. In fact, I went through a period in high school when I would go into Tatum's drugstore on the Decatur, Georgia, town square after baseball practice, sit at the soda fountain, order a fountain Pepsi, drink a little bit out of it, lean over the counter (surreptitiously or not, depending on who the incumbent soda jerk was), squirt a little extra Pepsi syrup or soda water into my glass, drink a little bit more, and go on topping up almost indefinitely. Meanwhile my teammates and I would wait for someone to drive the wrong way around the square so that we could run outside and shout, *"Are you CRAZY?! You're going around the square backward!"* This was in many ways a gratifying time in my life. It is worth noting, however, that Tatum's did not serve fountain Coke. I always thought Coke had more edge, more snap. My assumption was that Pepsi wished it had access to Coke's secret ingredient, so that it could taste more like Coke. I regarded Pepsi as Cokesque. Coke *invented* cola, right? In recent years I have ceased to drink cola, except occasionally when I feel bad. I prefer seltzer, beer, rum, orange juice, wine, gin, cold water, grape juice, vodka, iced tea (*not* canned), margaritas, eggnog, stout, buttermilk, pineapple juice, slivovitz, ale, coffee, grapefruit juice, cognac, and limeade. Compared to any of these beverages, cola now tastes gucky to me. Among colas, however, the old Coke seemed least gucky. When I found out that Coke wanted to be more like Pepsi instead of the other way around, a small but long-standing aspect of my worldview turned upside down. Next you'll be telling me something really devastating—that Louis Armstrong always wanted to play more like Al Hirt.

Is it fair to describe Coke's new taste as flatter, sweeter, more like Pepsi?

The Coca-Cola Company says no. Committed Coke drinkers of my acquaintance say yes. One thing that everyone, except oenologists, might agree on: The tongue and palate, essential as they are to both language and gustation, cannot produce words for what anything—except sugar, salt, sour cream, fish in general, and defeat—tastes like.

Is there anything that ought, *for the sake of world betterment, to be more like Pepsi?*
How about cocaine? This is not likely to happen, however, because it would cause cocaine to lose market points.

If Coke Is It, and also was *It, and in between they have changed it, what does it mean to say "it" anymore?*

DOGS VIS-À-VIS CATS

Which is the better pet, a cat or a dog?

Well, which is the better fruit, an apple or an orange?

Of dogs, in my time, I have had Sailor, Brownie, Bobby, Smokey, Butch, Snoopy (before "Peanuts"), Tubby, Sam, Chipper, Owen, Peggy, Ned, Sadie, Mollie and Pie. Of cats, I have had Stranger, Lulu, Angel, Emmy, Piedmont, Haile, Bale, Snope and Eloise. And Peggy's eight puppies and Eloise's two batches of kittens.

Down through the years, those hairy little entities have been parts of my life, nearly as intimate to me as my ankles. I have predominantly fond thoughts about every one of them, except possibly Smokey, who used to get lost and have to be bailed out of the pound all the time.

In the presence of all those names, I hate to generalize. Emmy acted a lot like a dog, and Tubby hung around happily with cats. You can't lump your pets together by their species any more than you can your friends by their professions. (I have known English professors who acted like people in the shrimping business.) But I'll tell you one thing. A cat can't smile. Or won't.

A dog will smile. Romp with your dog for a while and he or she will beam. Light up. You tell me the expression on that dog's face is not a smile. A mule or a monkey or a porpoise will sort of grin, but a dog is the only animal that will *smile*.

I'm not saying a cat won't joke. One morning I came downstairs to find a whole, perfect, upright rabbit's head on the floor. It looked as though a rabbit had stuck its head up through the floor to take a look around. Only the head wasn't moving.

"Waughh!" was my first reaction. Then I realized that a perky-looking disembodied rabbit's head on the floor was Snope's or Eloise's idea of a joke. Neither of them would own up to it in any way, of course. Neither of them smiled. I love cats but . . . But I am always saying, "I love cats, but . . ."

A dog will make eye contact. A cat will, too, but a cat's eyes don't even look entirely warm-blooded to me, whereas a dog's eyes look human except less guarded. A dog will look at you as if to say, "What do you want me to do for you? I'll do anything for you." Whether a dog *can* in fact, do anything for you if you don't have sheep (I never have) is another matter. The dog is *willing.*

A cat will do something for you: a cat will mouse. But I'm not sure that a house free of mice is better off than a house free of kitty litter. (I hate kitty litter. Have you ever been washing your hands and had your wet bar of soap fall into the kitty litter? Or your toothbrush? In the morning?) And a cat that mouses will also gerbil, parakeet, and rabbit. Furthermore, a cat will not do any of these things because you want him to.

I say that from experience and observation. I say it in the face of recent comments by Dr. Michael W. Fox, the scientific director of the Humane Society of the U.S. Fox maintains that he knows of cats that switch on lights, cats that flush the toilet, cats that press the lever of an electric can opener, and one cat that "knocks the telephone off the hook when it rings, listens to the receiver and meows into the mouthpiece." He cites another cat that would only take a pill "after its owner told it the pill was important to take."

Okay. Okay. After its owner told it the pill was *important to the cat.* You won't find a cat that will do something because it means a great deal to the owner.

When a cat makes eye contact with a person, the cat's expression says, "So?" There is little that a person can say in response to this expression. Cats have not forgotten that they were worshiped by the ancient Egyptians. It went to their heads. A cat's eyes know what a cat's eyes know.

Dogs' eyes twinkle, well up, express yearning. Which may be why cats are fast overtaking dogs in popularity in American homes. Taking care of cats is less of a problem than taking care of dogs, and cats are less demanding *emotionally*. A dog will smile, and a dog will also look at you as if you have been abusing him because you have not kneaded the place where his ears join onto his head in the last ten minutes. "Is it something I did?" the dog's eyes ask. "Haven't I been a good enough dog to you? God knows you know I love you. Why don't you want to go out into the woods and watch me chase squirrels? You're breaking—I'm not *accusing* you. I know you must have a reason, but I'm just saying—you're breaking my heart." Having a dog in the home is too much like having a person. Having a cat in the home is not enough like having a person.

Robert Graves once said that he wrote novels for the money he needed to live so he could write poetry. His books or prose, he said, were the show dogs he raised to support his cat. I guess a cat is sort of like a poem. A cat is relatively short. A cat is only subtly demonstrative. To be sure, you can curl up with a good cat, but that doesn't mean you *understand* the cat. A dog is like Dickens.

WHAT GUYS CAN'T STAND

Passions? Here are things that guys,
Deep down inside, *despise*.

Tiny things they can't pick up.
Not your proverbial porcelain cup
So much as, you know, *nuance*. "Um,
I'm full of loving. You want some?"
A guy may say in a spirit of gen-
Erosity, and smile, and then:
Uh-oh. Missed some small "relation-
Ship" kind of consideration,
Which she now builds an opus on.
A guy named Guy de Maupassant
Wrote a story, "The Piece of String":
It's always some *little* thing.

That's why guys have broad-based doubts
Regarding angel hair and sprouts.
Don't eat anything thinner than rice
Is good solid guys' advice.

Something else guys can't abide
Is patience. Guys have tried and tried
To sit . . . still . . . and not to fidget
Or snore at some damn four-digit-

Ticket beaux arts gala affair;
Tried to deliberate over her hair;
Tried to creep at 55 or
So behind a cowering driver . . .
Guys can't. They want to get
A move on. To where they aren't to yet.

The converse of that is, say a guy sits
For six straight hours drinking Schlitz
And watching football. Say he does.
Does he need to hear the buzz
Of criticism round his head
From those who wish he were instead
The kind of guy who plays recorder
En famille with wife and dorder?
No. He doesn't need to hear it.
He is with the girls in spirit.

Guys can't fathom women's tears.
They may have a couple beers
And get misty in their fashion,
But a woman goes into such an *irration-*
Al state it's *scary* when she cries.
At worst, it's a face-in-the-chili with guys.
Where do women think they get
The right to be so damn upset?
What if guys got that undone?
It makes guys want to hit someone.

Another thing that's always bugged
Guys: the threat of being mugged.
In jail, the street, commerce, court,
Marriage, politics, or sport.
Bad enough losing, therefore owing
Another meal to sharks and going

Unloved or else unfitly loved—
To think of having something *shoved* . . .
Guys hate that. Otherwise
They'd do it less to other guys.

Guys would rather suck dry ice
Than stick to saying something nice.
Guys grow up exchanging whacks
And slurs; they seldom wax
Supportive quite convincingly
(Wary of coming off mincingly)
Unless, that is, testosterone
Whispers, "Don't go home alone!
Get yourself cracking after
Her, there. Say whate'er you hafter,
And mean it. For the time being.
Tell her, 'You're like Venus, skiing. . . .' "

Of course, no given guy's generic—
Ollie North to David Merrick,
Each one has his own bêtes noires,
From bigotry to Asian cars.
Which doesn't mean that mine should be
Associated just with me.
Still, I think that I can state
That one thing I and all guys hate
Is guys who, well, equivocate.

Then too, all this is changing. Guys
Are learning now to sensitize,
Come alive and join the Eighties,
Act like human beings (ladies
Is roughly what is meant by that).
Guys today are sweet to a cat
And take an interest in curtains. But

If there's one thing that guys have gut
Adverse reactions to, it is
To read a column (headed "His")
In which they're told they're sensitizing.
And guys can't stand, in advertising,
Guys shown being so damn guysome. . . .
Must we watch these scenes? I'll buy some
Löwenbräu if Löwenbräu'll
Show me Adam Clayton Powell,
To take a name just from the blue,
Or Pelé, or Gérard Depardieu,
Or William Powell, or Bud, or Dick—
Guys who do not make me sick.
Where do they get these guys? L.A.?
What gets guys' goats is guys manqué.

THE WIND REWOUND

. . . . .

Gone with the Wind is a novel of war and Reconstruction. The sequel, working title *Fiddle-dee-dee*, begins as a novel of pique and deconstruction.

It is either 1980 or 1890, and a frowsy, dispirited Scarlett is cranking out a metafictional memoir of her declining years—or is she? Certainly the characters keep talking back to her, calling her wayward and headstrong and coquettish, but does she put these words into their mouths or do they speak them of their own accord so as to cast their narrator in a more interesting light? Whatever is going on, it is a mess and a disgrace, and nobody is making any bones about *that* except old General Reader, a recurrent voice reduced to a litany of "Sho nuff, I reckon. I don't rightly know."

Rhett is a character-within-a character (for one thing, people keep asking him whether people ever tell him he looks like Clark Gable), who is determined to get out of character altogether. He fancies himself an earnest but ineffective reformer—he wears an anachronistic (whichever year it is) "Give a Damn" button and a T-shirt that says *"Today* Is Another Day." But Scarlett stamps her foot and won't hear of it.

"I'll tell you what your trouble is, Scahlett," he says. "You think you're omniscient."

"She's not even the first person," sniffs Belle Watling, who is tired of being essentially good-natured after all these years, and owns hotels.

"Lawsy, Miss Scahlit, I don't know nothin' 'bout bein' no stereotype, I am a human being with my own inner feelings and aspirations, or am I jus' li'l blips of ink?" Prissy says.

Ashley Wilkes has gone and gotten so sicklied o'er with the pale cast of thought that he has decided nobody can say anything that signifies anything substantial to anybody else. And that's exactly what he keeps telling everybody all the time.

Aunt Pittypat, become extremely literary, exists only to toss in remarks like "The authuh of *Black Mischief* on his way home from Brideshead. Give up? Waugh between estates."

Melanie sports an adjustable cap that says "Too Sweet for Words" and has taken to going out and shooting everyone she can find in a blue suit.

The only character who acts like herself is Mammy, who keeps walking in on whiny self-referential goings-on and stomping right back out again saying, "Hunh! Ain't fittin'!"

Finally Scarlett has had enough. She summons all her resources, gets down on the floor of her burnt-out study, digs elbow-deep into drifts of blighted barren manuscript, and utters a vow: "As God is my witness, I am going to take ahold of this pore sorry mealymouth material here and turn it into a novel of *real epic sweep,* like in the old days!"

And she does.

I just don't know how.

SHOE-SHOEING LIT

My daddy down in Georgia told me, "Son, take pride in your work, don't honk at old people, and never read a Civil War novel longer than *The Red Badge of Courage.*"

So I never did. Until *High Hearts,* by Rita Mae Brown. I'd been meaning to read her earlier novels, which I'd heard were roguish and good. The premise of this one seemed promising: Geneva, the heroine, cuts her hair and enlists in the Confederate cavalry as a man so that she can be near her husband, who turns out not to be her equal as a warrior. Threatening to me, as a former indifferent male soldier; but hey, I can be threatened.

I've heard that Rita Mae Brown is a witty and engaging speaker, and in her pictures she looks like she'd be a fun person to be in the cavalry with. Daddy can't have anticipated a writer who used to keep company with the best women's tennis player in the world; who is on record as also liking men; who helped found the radical feminist group, Redstockings; who had an Amish father and a Southern mother; who studied English and classics at NYU; who served on the Literature Panel of the National Endowment for the Arts; who holds a Ph.D. from the Institute for Policy Studies.

So I broke Daddy's rule.

I read faster and faster, wishing I could read faster still; driving, driving; wiping away bad black English, caked blood, good Virginia soil, and bad white English; pausing only to note that at three different points in the first eighty-one pages someone was described as not having the sense God gave a goose. It's a good expression, but it can be overworked.

So can dangling modifiers. If you took them out of the following passage, I realize, you would have to go in and completely rewrite, thereby endangering several subtle inadvertent effects:

"Steam moistened Geneva's nostrils as she gulped her hot chocolate. Expensive and delicious, Geneva preferred this luxury to jewelry, but Lutie assured her that as she grew older, she'd develop a taste for stones."

But you don't want to run dangling modifiers into the ground, page in and page out. "Shod a week ago, these shoes fit him perfectly." I wonder whether any former member of the Literture Panel of the National Endowment for the Arts has shod shoes, publicly, before.

Geneva gets to do a lot of neat stuff (which she later comes to recognize as part of man's inhumanity to man): engage in fistfights, blow Yankees away, chop down telegraph poles. In battle, the good guys tend to have catlike reflexes. I kept being reminded of baseball books for boys. I have never read a novel by John Jakes, but this is what I imagine one is like. You have heard about the influence of movies on the novel. This is an example of the influence of miniseries.

The dialogue would chip a beaver's teeth. One belle to another. "Sin-Sin was impressed when Evangelista guided her through your labyrinthine closets and showed her every gown for which you've marked a card stating when you wore it, where you wore it, and what shoes, hat, gloves and parasol you wore with it."

This is the only novel I have ever read in whose acknowledgments cats are thanked ("my mews: Cazenovia, Sneaky Pie, Pewter, and Buddha") *and* in whose text a mother, unhinged by grief, seizes her son's severed head and tries to eat it. Trying times.

Another character makes a true observation: "Man can live without pleasure, but doan know if he can live without the future." Not for long, anyway.

You are young. I have lived through 464 pages of the past and the past perfect, indiscriminately mixed. *Listen to me.* I don't care who wrote it, don't read a Civil War novel longer than *The Red Badge of Courage*.

REB BANNER UNLOADED

. . . . . .

Stokely Carmichael hustles some kind of tedious pan-African socialism now, I believe, but in his day he was a lively American. My friend Bruce Tucker recalls seeing him speak at Vanderbilt in 1967. Someone in the balcony unfurled an enormous Confederate flag.

"That's all right," Carmichael said. "That's cool. You got a right to show a flag." Pause. "But don't you be bombing my churches."

Looking back on it now, "my" churches was maybe a bit thick, since I don't think Carmichael was ever much of a Baptist. But it wasn't anywhere near as thick as that damn-fool flag. Which did, after all, evoke church-bombing, God help it. And which, on this occasion, was meekly refurled.

Let us leave it that way.

1. When was the last time the Confederate flag had a glorious moment?

2. It's a white people's flag. And the South is not exclusively a white people's place. (I've *lived* in white people's places. Western Connecticut. You think pan-African socialism is tedious.)

3. Any flag serves more as a chip on the shoulder than as anything else.

Instinctively, I defend the South. (Except when I'm in the South.) I even have a grindingly ambivalent taste for Nathan

Bedford Forrest. But the Confederate flag is something I have not felt a shred of affection for since, oh, roughly, puberty.

And yet I got into a temper over it recently with a Northern friend. She said her sister, on a visit to Atlanta, had objected to seeing the Rebel colors flying over Georgia's capitol. My friend, being better informed, had assured her sister that this was in fact the Georgia state flag, with a vertical band of blue on it. "I didn't see any band of blue," her sister had said, in tones of outrage.

This came up when I mentioned I was writing about the Confederate flag. "I can tell you that Northerners are offended by it," my friend told me.

And I saw red. "Well *know* a lot of Northerners," I said in the Biblical sense.

Thereby leaving myself wide open. If she had come back with "Teach your grandmother to suck eggs," I'd've been outflanked even by my own standards.

Instead, she responded in one of those provoking, reasonable-sounding ways. "Why does the South need a flag?" she asked. "The *North* doesn't have a flag."

I could have spurred my charger. "That's because the North isn't a place," I could have cried. "It's just a direction out of the South."

But I didn't. The night before, I had gotten overwrought in resistance to this same friend's contention that she had no accent. I hate it when people start an argument and then sit there, not even acknowledging that there *is* an argument, watching me get more and more stereotypical. I have a strong enough tendency to get recalcitrant when Northerners say things about the South, even when I agree with them. I don't need to be wasting powder and shot over the damn Confederate flag.

"The point is," I told her, "that Southern black people are offended by it."

And so am I.

This issue is dumb, but it must be real. It keeps arising.

In May 1986, black politicians in Memphis induced a Beale Street saloonkeeper to take the Confederate flag down off his wall. In protest, two white men draped themselves in it and walked up and down Beale Street. My people, my people.

And last fall, the NAACP demonstrated at a football game at South Grand Prairie High School, in Texas, because the white students were whipping up their rah-rahs by brandishing the Beauregard battle flag. (That's what it is. People call it the Stars and Bars, but that was an earlier version; that banner was replaced by General P.G.T. Beauregard after troops kept getting it confused with the Stars and Stripes at the first battle of Manassas.)

We're talking about a banner under which 200,000 men died, a big percentage of them slowly, with scant attention, in defense of secession, which was a bad idea even then. Southern white rooters persist in bandying the damn thing about. And authorities generally have to command them, as they did in Grand Prairie, to stop.

Adolescence is complicated enough as it is. Young people need something to flaunt that does not combine, historically, slavery and failed independence. Truck drivers need bumper stickers and license plates (Confederate ones are big sellers) that don't raise tensions on the highways.

Every flag is loaded, but this one, whether its champions realize it or not (and many of them do), is loaded with anti-integrationism. Whatever your politics are, I don't see how you can disagree that a flag ought to bring the people under it together. A confederacy is a union. The Confederacy was a regional union. A regional union that repels those citizens of the region without whom there would have been no cotton or rock 'n' roll—or any Atlanta, as we know it—is pretty sorry.

Let us assume that there is some point, in this day and age, to a flag of the South. And let us assume that people want one for other than racist reasons.

Let us come up with a flag that a Southerner with *sense* can salute.

I can't draw or sew, so I guess I'm not the one to produce the new design. I'm a word person, and one who has always felt that Southerners stand most tall when they aren't being obvious about it, so I'd probably just suggest a blue background (for the blues, which are the wellspring of Southern, hence American, culture) with a slogan on it: something like "Just a Pretty Good Country Part of the Country." But then Southern business would point out that nobody can make any money out of the blues.

I might emphasize food. A nice baked sweet potato with the jacket open on top and a pat of butter melting in it, over the words "Don't Tread on Me." But then the peach and okra growers would get their backs up.

So how about this: half the background's blue, and other half green, for money. And against that background we see, not vegetables, but something real human: hands. A dark brown woman's hand, an about-the-same-color man's hand, a tanned white man's hand, and an about-the-same-color woman's hand.

The hands ought to look strong, but peaceable. Hands clearly capable of making a fist, but not naturally clenched. What ought those hands to be doing? Well, what does a flag do? What do folks in the South often do in moments of good feeling? Those hands ought to be waving.

And let's do have a few words. People in the South distinctively enjoy words. There ought not to be so many words that people with something to do would walk off in the middle of them, but enough words to be sociable. There ought to be a slogan on the flag that is proud but not swaggering, clever but not letting on, truly polite but not truly humble, outgoing but sufficiently selfish.

How about this? "Just Fine, and You?"

FILOFAX FEVER

*"Everyone has enough money,
but nobody has enough time."*
*—Helene Furst,
Londonhouse Corporation,
U.S. agent for Filofax*

What we are seeing is that people are beginning to perceive either themselves or their Filofaxes—the distinction is not crucial—as breaking down. Not mechanically. Everyone is still working out, and Filofaxes' ring still snap shut like a Mercedes door. But conceptually. Let's listen in.

"I had the ultimate self-management system," says H.L. (not her real initials) of New York. "Utilizing inserts by Day-Timers, Day Runner, Lefax, I.D/Design, Bond Street, Mundi, Sandi's Super System, and Rio dè USA, as well as self-created ones like my 'How My Face Is Looking' table calibrated from PUFFY to HAGGARD in intervals of tenths of an hour, I had all my personal, physical, business, and spiritual concerns organized at the flip of a few pages and all *handily portable* in basic caressable Filofax-blue calf.

"And yet . . ."

"I was keeping bees in mine," says Kim of the U.K.

"How do you mean, 'keeping bees in it'?" asks the group facilitator, but his voice is drowned out.

"I had it all," says Gary of Cincinnati (yes, *Cincinnati*). "Four hundred different inserts, many of them leaves that opened to double, triple, and quad length, in twenty-four different colors. Before, I'd never known there *were* so many colors. Now there were not only these new colors in my life but also 1,638 employees whom I'd hired (I'm a mason) just because I found I could keep track of them and their performance with such ease. And yet . . ."

"I guess it was sort of like that old saying," says someone else, "I got my shit together, and then I couldn't lift it."

"No, that's not—"

"*Physically* I could lift it. Physically I had it all there, my life: it really only weighed seventeen ounces. Because for all the incredible wealth of ordered detail, the pages, though durable and erasable, were—if not of onionskin, for tracing—of premium banker's bond: light, so light, yet so strong. And yet—"

"I had one Filofax for actual daily life, one for *me* that made it easier to like myself, one for the IRS, and one for posterity. All photocopied hourly in case of loss or theft," says D'Arcy of Connecticut.

Which brings up another problem: what we have been finding is that the criminal element is getting involved. Muggers originally took Filofaxes only for resale, but then they started thinking, *Hey, no wonder these people are better off than me. This thing could pull my whole operation together.* So now we have scum budgeting time for drugs, running, downtime, viciousness. The perfect productivity tool turned to evil purposes.

And yet, says Norton of Westchester, "evil wasn't the problem. I had a tabbed divider for EVIL. I had EVIL no more or less in hand than APPOINTMENTS. The problem was TIME."

"No, it was AGENDA. AGENDA became an end in itself. *Sheer* agenda."

"Oh, I could lift it, all right. I could carry my shit anywhere, even into the pool. But it was as if my shit—"

"Time," says Liz of L.A., a macroeconomist, "*is* the problem. I own, *on paper,* an absolute *age*—but when can I spend that time? I find myself devoting too much time to saving time. Turning time over. Moving great blocks of time from one color-coded . . ."

And, of course, Filofaxes fell into the hands of madmen.

"Well, I wouldn't say 'madman,' " says I.L. of Atlanta. "But you know my daddy sits around all day believing he's a Confederate general? He was doing it way back before Ceil gave him that Filofax for Christmas. But it seems like now that he can run three campaigns at one time and remember exactly when and why he gave each of his lieutenants a rawhiding or a pat on the back . . . Well, it gives him more time to call in to the radio shows, and that in turn gets him so worked up because he'll start tearing into Jeff Davis's interference and hollering about Shiloh, and when they cut him off he calls me up and says, 'It's here in muh appointment book. It's right here, I could show it to um. It's as plain as day!' And it is too."

"Not only did I have my shit together, but in ostrich-grain Italian pigskin—"

"Did you have Velcro closure?"

"Of course I had Velcro closure. Specially adapted for my needs. I had my shit together in ostrich-grain Italian pigskin with specially adapted Velcro closure right there in my suit-coat pocket. I could *feel* it, I swear, *throbbing* in there."

No sooner are people on top of their priorities, it seems, than their priorities are on top of them. And you know human nature.

"We were a one-Filofax family. But you know how kids are. Testing, always testing. They would come and ask to borrow it for a weekend. So we got them each a Play Runner by Harper House, with its colorful five-tab section, ziplock pouch, neon ruler, and over seventy-five illustrated labels allowing children to make special places for everything from FIELD TRIPS to FRIENDS to HEROES. And my wife got to the point that she wanted sex only when it *wasn't* booked. So how could we book it?" says Porter of Boston.

"I had my shit together and—"

"I had a section for PASSION," says Maeve of Sydney (Australia). "But when I turned to it, it was there, but I was . . . spent."

". . . Throbbing in my suit-coat pocket. But was it *my* shit? Was it *its* shit? Was it shit as we have known it, or was it some new form of shit that perhaps required a whole new mastery system? And would this system, in turn—"

"Let's get back to this woman over here," says the group facilitator. "Do you mean you were keeping *actual bees* in yours?"

III.

SHOW AND TELL

OF THE EFFABLE

"**B**ut, of course," Arthur Quinn writes in his book *Figures of Speech*, "there are few things about which more has been said and written than the ineffable."

Among those few things, we might assume, is the effable. But do we, in fact, speak or write about the effable, *as such*, very often? Don't we rather take it for granted? And yet—shall I compare the effable to a summer's day? No, for the effable is so much more referential.

Without the ineffable we could get along. In fact, we would have a far clearer notion of what, if anything, we were trying to get along to. But where would we be without the effable? We would be constantly moping or musing (hard to tell which), like certain people I could name; no, thank you.

Of course you can say that everything is ultimately (so to speak) ineffable: that to keep on focusing harder, as we for some ineffable reason do, is to see every solution dissolve. But when you've said that, you've said a mouthful.

Some effable things:
- Cheerfulness.
- Making a deal, sticking to it.
- Pitter-patter of little feet.
- The pertinence here of the euphemism "effing."
- Footsie.
- The blues.

WHERE I GET MY IDEAS

I think if it were revealed to us how we really think, we would be struck dumb. A tape recorder wired directly into the RUT (Raw, Unprocessed Thought) center of the brain would pick up none of your "Hmmm, mebbe I better turn this one over in the old noggin" or "Got . . . to . . . get . . . hands . . . free . . . before . . . fumes . . . reach . . ."

No, the actual stuff of thought consists of particles far more confounding than words, far more elementary than anything Sherlock Homes deduced, far less composed than strangled cries, even. The blither, the glitch, the uh-oh, the meemee, the ravelet, the huh?, the holyjump, the "nntab" (for "no, not that, anything but"), the oohah, the flinch, the urgh, the umyamama: These are but vague and dainty approximations of the crazed, unwashed, slavering, half-naked sub-blips that careen, gobble, and interbreed along the space-time continuum of what we so blithely call the human noodle.

And yet, when I go out on the road to promote a book I have written, people ask me briskly, "Where do you get your ideas?"

This matter—like how sausage is made—is one I don't like to dwell on. I feel about writing the way a struggling designated hitter once told me he felt about batting: "I think too much at the plate. I ought to be just stupid up there."

"Just see the idea and hit it" is my motto. And yet I find myself wondering whether my noun is cocked right, when to shift my weight forward onto my predicate, how I can keep my "of"s and "the"s down.

Say a compulsion wells up in me to render an utterance that settles once and for all the question of Why Most People Look Sad. Let the critics pick apart the hitches in my swing later. I just want to explode. I want the ball to leap off the bat. It is not my job to watch where it lands, even. I just want to feel the sweet spots mesh and then go into my trot.

The last thing I want to be smart about is where my ideas come from. People don't ask George Will where his bow tie comes from; it is just there when he needs it, so far. It was not *my* idea, in the first place, to be the kind of person to whom ideas come. Some people get eczema, I get ideas.

Still, there I am on the radio in, say, Someplace, Ohio. The studio clock is reeling in expensive seconds, and under that clock hangs a sign that says " Be Interesting." My job is to stimulate several people to rush out and buy my book, whether they will like it or not. And some listener calls in—from a traffic jam, a crawl space, a telephone pole—and inquires, "I was just wondering. Where do you get your ideas?"

And I just say, "Uh."

I am never welcomed back to the airwaves of Somewhere.

So not long ago, I decided that the next time I felt what might be an idea coming on, I would keep track of it.

And I did.

One day I was standing in a country store near where I live. I will not give the name of this store, lest someone be inspired to build condominiums next to it. But is is a place where I feel at ease, a place I go into nearly every day when I am not out on the road making appearances. A place where I do not feel obliged to be apparent.

I was standing there looking for baking soda. Or at least I thought I was looking for baking soda. Actually I was standing there in a fog.

A person who gets ideas is often in a fog. This may cause such a person to stumble. To drop something. To step on a baby on the beach. Or just to be "standing there, dead to the world," as my mother used to say regarding me. A woman once told me that she hurt her back just before a long-awaited trip to Europe, so that when she stood at last in the Sistine Chapel she was unable to look up. It would not surprise me, or anyone who has traveled with me, if I were to stand in the Sistine Chapel and just neglect to look up, because I am in a fog. Whether Michelangelo was ever in a fog (to look at Charlton Heston playing him, you wouldn't think so), I don't know, but then I am not in the visual arts.

"Where's the baking soda?" I asked.

I do not know who answered. It may have been David or Barbara Lowman, the store's proprietors, or it may have been one of the many voices of schizophrenia. The answer, at any rate, was:

"It's right in front of your nose. If it'd been a snake, it would've bit you."

Whether this was sufficient to direct my attention to the baking soda, I don't at this point recall. I know that it made me start thinking about the expression "If it'd been a snake, it would've bit you."

An expression that I have heard many times over the years. I come from the South, where expressions are rife. "Grinning like a cat eating yellow jackets." "Crazy as a road lizard." Living in New England, as I do, I don't hear many expressions. When they do arise, even old familiar ones, I linger over them.

That, it struck me, is exactly what I want to come up with: an idea so self-evident that, once stated, it causes people to think, "If that idea had been a snake, it would've bit me." To be the first person to strike upon such an idea—or to be struck by it—is my desire.

Take *"Cogito, ergo sum."* Bingo. Why didn't *I* think of that? The most obvious thing in the world, when you think about it.

My problem is, if such an idea ever did occur to me, I would probably think right past it. "I think, therefore I am. I think."

The next day I was flying through Atlanta. That is, I was in the Atlanta airport, changing planes. The Atlanta airport is not a fertile field for expressions, because its tone is dominated by mechanical voices.

There is the quasi-lilting female voice that says:

"You . . . are . . . now . . . approaching . . . the . . . endless . . . walkway. . . . Please . . . keep . . . to . . . your . . . right . . . so . . . that . . . those . . . passengers . . . driven . . . insane . . . by . . . this . . . sound track . . . may . . . bolt . . . and . . . run."

Then there is the bloodless sort-of-male voice that says: "You . . . have . . . boarded . . . the . . . miracle . . . electronic . . . shuttle . . . train. . . . That . . . passenger . . . who . . . has . . . allowed . . . some . . . portion . . . of . . . his . . . or . . . her . . . body . . . or . . . carry-on . . . luggage . . . to . . . block . . . the . . . miracle . . . electronic . . . sliding . . . door . . . will . . . remove . . . it . . . now . . . please. . . . Or . . . we . . . will . . . be . . . here . . . all . . . night. . . . It . . . is . . . all . . . the . . . same . . . to . . . me."

Is there any hope for this couple? Perhaps in the depths of night, when the airport empties, those two voices get together:

"I . . . thought . . . they . . . would . . . never . . . leave."

"Isn't . . . it . . . the . . . truth."

And in time the voices will have issue. You know how radically successive generations depart. Perhaps a new wave of voices loaded with feeling will crop up around the terminal.

Exultant:

Sing hallelujah, you're in the cocktail lounge!

Or bluesy:

Here is the newsstand, get a
Paper or a candy bar.

> *Lord, Lord.*
> *Here is the newsstand, get a*
> *Paper or a candy bar.*
> *Neither one ever done nobody*
> *No good so far.*

Protesting, even:

> *I ain't got no message on*
> *That white courtesy telephone.*

Until that day comes, unlively language will prevail in the Atlanta airport. I did, however, overhear one man there who spoke from the heart. "The way she ignored me," he said, "you'd think I was a tree stump."

I bore that expression in mind as I boarded my flight to wherever I was going and took a window seat. Not my usual practice. I am too jaded an air traveler to relish the view of whole cities and natural wonders spread out as if by magic below me. My usual practice is to take an aisle seat so I can get to the rest room quickly. (And incidentally: What is this peremptory RETURN TO YOUR SEAT sign that lights up the first hint of turbulence? They can't put a belt on the seat you've got right there?)

But the nonsmoking aisles had all been reserved, so I took the window.

An elegant Frenchwoman sat down beside me. Her legs were long and in a dusky sort of hose. When she spoke to a baby in the row ahead, her accent and perhaps her words (it was hard to tell, since she was addressing a baby) were French. She was carrying a book in the popular but distinguished *Livre de Poche* series. French, then, I gathered. And elegant.

I wanted her to have a good impression of America. So often foreigners make snap judgments about this country, when what do they know, really? "You Americans all have extremely good teeth," an Englishman once informed me magisterially, "because you drink quantities of milk."

"Well, kiss my ass," I told him.

It was my intention to be a good—a surprisingly not-so-simple—ambassador to this Frenchwoman. Impart to her a sense of America as a country of many shades, levels, and, yes, nuances. I considered how I could best begin to go about this.

And then in the aisle seat arrived a faceless businessman. Have you ever wondered who the in-flight magazine is edited for? There he was. Tan poplin suit, green tie with spermatozoa on it, boxy briefcase. The American flier. Just by looking at him I could tell he was going to do something that would cause this elegant Frenchwoman to nod knowingly to herself. I had to head off this . . . this *type*.

But before I could get started, the stewardess offered us drinks, and here is what the aisle man did:

Ordered a Coke. Opened his briefcase. Drew from within it a Milky Way bar. Which he unwrapped and dunked into the Coke.

Now, I am from Georgia. I did not grow up with haute cuisine. But I know better than to eat like that. I could just hear this Frenchwoman back home (my translation): "America is a land where . . . I tell you how best to put it: What they eat is a chocolate bar soaked in Coca-Cola."

Now I had to do something quick. I turned to her with an offhand gesture.

I myself had ordered a glass of sipping whiskey, a tasteful choice. As I gestured, I hit that drink with my hand.

There is something about those flimsy plastic glasses in which you are served drinks on airplanes: They want to fly up into the air. That's what this one did. But over the years a person who gets ideas develops a good second move. I have developed a knack for catching things, or myself. For instance, I have never put my full weight down on a baby on the beach.

I caught my drink of whiskey. Pretty cleanly. There was some slosh, but not much. I still felt possessed of savoir faire. I turned toward the elegant Frenchwoman again.

I don't know whether you have had this experience (I had had it, but it had slipped my mind): When you spill whiskey on one of those airplane tray tables, it creates a film. And when you set one of those skittery plastic cups down on it, the cup tends to creep.

So it was that when I gestured toward the Frenchwoman a second time, my drink had worked its way into the path of my hand again. And my drink went straight up into the air again.

A person can do such a thing once. When he does it twice, it may seem to be a folkway. A kind of savage rite. "America is . . . how shall I say? On airplanes, 50 percent of Americans eat chocolate bars soaked in Coca-Cola, and the other 50 percent attempt to attract the attention of women by knocking glasses of whiskey into the air."

This time the slosh was greater. I don't think much got on her, but a great deal did on me. The aisle man made a show of coming to my aid with a (chocolate-stained) handkerchief, which I waved away—in the process sending my drink aloft one last time.

As I dabbed myself with *USA Today* (which I must say is not very absorbent), I sought the words to explain.

But when I turned to her once again, her back was turned to me as squarely as an elegant back can be in such close quarters. She was giving all her attention to the man with the Milky Way. Purely in the interest of research, I feel sure, but still it hurt.

And so I turned to ideas.

Having failed to please in life (in wine, in women), I fell back toward song.

I thought of what I had heard the man in the airport say. And a line came:

She just seems to think I'm a tree stump.

Fine. But where to go from there? I ran into a scarcity of rhymes for "tree stump." With some strain, I pictured a man in a clerical collar batting in a softball game and being called out on strikes. He turns to the secular arbiter behind him, and appeals:

> *Have a heart—you know I'm a priest, Ump.*

No flies on that rhyme qua rhyme, but priests and softball did not easily fit into my concept.

So I sighed, and flashed back farther. To the country store. And the whole song burst into being:

> *Darling tell me why*
> *I can't catch your eye*
> *How can I get you*
> *To admit you*
> *Saw me standing here*
> *Grinning ear to ear?*
> *If I was a snake I'da bit you.*

So there you go. Now when people ask me where I get my ideas, I begin to cite that example. And soon they change the subject.

INCONGRUOUS "WE"

. . . .

The most vexed, loaded, and crucial word of the United States Constitution is a two-letter word that I used too blithely, once, in argument with a friend of mine.

"Who is this 'we'?" he responded. "You got a mouse in your pocket?"

What I meant by that particular *we*, presumably, was "I and also you, if I can slip this by you." The *we* of "We the People"—a phrase that offended Patrick Henry, startled many Constitutional Convention delegates, and helped inspire the French Revolution—is a somewhat more complicated proposition.

Webster's Third quotes this *we* as an illustration of the following definition: "I and the rest of a group that includes me: you and I: you and I and another or others: I and another or others not including you." Confusing enough for most of us, but not for Ambrose Bierce, who wrote in *The Devil's Dictionary* that the plural of *I* "is said to be *we*, but how there can be more that one myself is doubtless clearer to the grammarians than it is to the author of this incomparable dictionary."

The Articles of Confederation, which the Constitution superseded, began: "To all to whom these Presents shall come, we the undersigned Delegates of the States affixed to our Names send greeting." A cheerier but far less subjective and audacious representation than "We the People of the United States do ordain and establish . . ."

Patrick Henry, who refused to take part in the Convention, was not the only patriot who saw tyranny lurking in that Preamble. A constitution with such a beginning "will effect a consolidation of the states under one government, which even the advocates of this Constitution admit, could not be done without the sacrifice of all liberty," declared dissenting members of the Pennsylvania delegation. That attitude persisted in the Reagan administration's allegiance to states' rights and corporations' prerogatives.

We could dispute the meaning of our primordial *we* endlessly, and in fact we do, increasingly in terms that would have confounded every mother's son among the Founding Fathers. "We the People" of 1787 was not *literally* racist: Some fifty thousand black freemen were included, as were, construably, Indians who were willing to be taxed. Or sexist: Nowhere in the Constitution was it written that only men could vote. But since the Constitution legitimized the existence of American slaves (referred to as "other persons"), and generally shunted aside Indians (itself a presumptuous term), and took for granted that women were not entitled to all the rights of citizenship, it certainly was discriminatory by assumption and in effect. And so is "We the People" of today, many of us *we*-sayers would say, thereby making many others of us feel insulted.

In 1984 the Democrats tried to proclaim their own *we*, which I personally found far less offensive than the Reagan *we*. But most of us voters disagreed with me. Every mainstream American political discourser tries to insinuate his or her (or, if you prefer, her or his) sense of *we* as the true American one. The Constitution's first-person-plural incongruities grind together and refine, slowly, its letter and its spirit.

What violates that spirit, it seems to me, is any exclusive, or *entre nous,* political *we,* when it is broadcast to the general public. In the early seventies, James Buckley ran as the Conservative candidate for the U.S. Senate in New York. His TV ads would close with, "Isn't it time *we* had a senator?"

This tagline outraged me, I told a conservative person I knew.

He snorted, and said liberals were always using *we* in the same gang-solipsistic way.

I suspected he might have a point, but I denied it. I said the essence of liberalism was that it spread things around. . . .

"After taking them from us," said the conservative.

. . . that it remembered the Forgotten Man . . .

"Assuming he votes Democratic."

. . . that it was open to the other . . .

"Assuming the Other is not conservative."

We agreed to disagree. But I did concede, in my heart, that he had a point—a liberal one. I didn't get the impression that he was willing to concede that I had a conservative one. And nowhere is it written that he had to.

Our Constitution is the first *written* national constitution in the world. Who can be called its authors? "We the People" (but not "of the United States") has been ascribed (but not with certainty) to James Wilson of Pennsylvania—which would make him America's most-quoted writer, at least this year. Had royalties been involved, perhaps some eighteenth-century equivalent of the Writers Guild of America would have adjudicated the question of which Constitutional delegates deserved how much writing credit. But probably not to anyone's perfect satisfaction.

James Madison's Virginia Plan pretty much set the Convention's agenda, but apparently more of the Constitution's language was lifted from principles set down by Charles Pinckney of South Carolina. What survives of the Pinckney Plan has been pieced together by historians, who have variously accused Pinckney of forging one version of it and Madison of suppressing significant mention of it.

We know that the Constitution's first working draft, which led off with "We the People," was produced by a five-man Committee of Detail, on which Wilson was prominent. After the Convention as a whole debated that draft for five weeks line by line, an entirely different five-man Committee of Style put the tentative consensus into literary form. Even Madison, who was a member of the Committee of Style, acknowledged Gouverneur Morris of Pennsylvania, a rakish, outspokenly irreligious lawyer, as the principal stylist. The Constitution "was written by the fingers that write this letter," Morris later wrote. It was Morris who decided—partly for tactical reasons—to follow "We the People of" with "the United States" instead of listing all the states individually as the Committee of Detail had done. (All five members of the Committee of Style were staunch Federalists. Morris, incidentally, spelled *federal, foederal.*)

Minor changes were made after further haggling among the delegates. The final alteration was, as George Mason of Virginia put it, "an Amendment, often before refused, and at last made by an Erasure, after the Engrossment upon Parchment, of the word *forty,* and inserting *thirty,* in the 3d Clause of the 2d Section of the 1st Article." The firm of Dunlap & Claypoole printed up five hundred copies. The Convention dissolved. Argument continued apace.

Solid, straightforward, unlegalistic as the Constitution generally is, it could have used a Committee of One Last Polish. Setting aside the glaring imperfections of pre-Constitution Union, how can anyone form "a more perfect Union"? *Webster's Third* cites the Preamble's usage of *perfect* as an illustration of this definition: "corresponding to an archetype; having all the proper characteristics: IDEAL." But strictly speaking, a thing can only be ideal or not ideal.

"A more nearly perfect Union"? Not heady enough. "A more viable Union"? Yuck. "A stronger Union"? That would have rattled the states'-righters' cage. "A Union with teeth"? "A Union that will fly"?

Let's let the preamble stand. It is certainly better written than the Bill of Rights, which was composed by Congress two years after the Convention ended. The Second Amendment has grave comma problems, and the First Amendment wouldn't get past a good newspaper's copy desk, which might mess up its rhythm by touching up its parallelism as follows:

"Congress shall make no law establishing any religion or prohibiting the free exercise thereof, or abridging either freedom of speech, freedom of the press, the right to assemble peaceably, or the right to petition the Government for redress of grievances."

I'll take the First Amendment the way it is, though, thank you. In fact I will take this occasion to quote it:

"Congress shall make no law respecting an establishment of religion, or prohibiting the free exercise thereof; or abridging the freedom of speech, or of the press; or the right of the people peaceably to assemble, and to petition the government for a redress of grievances."

It's our First Amendment, and it guarantees every American's right to say, for instance, of Ronald Reagan, "I have never had any use for the son of a bitch."

THE WIT AND WISDOM OF RONALD REAGAN

*(Note: This piece first appeared when the man
was still president. Of the United States!)*

O nly a sage or a nincompoop could look as cheerful about himself as the president does, and if he were a nincompoop, that would mean that the great majority of American voters have been nincompoops. It is clear that the president has the wit and the wisdom to know how laughable an idea that is.

But we should not take that wit and wisdom for granted. Since they have become so much a part of us, we owe it to ourselves to examine what they are made of. Let us consider some of their common hallmarks.

Simplicity

At a rally in Cincinnati in August of 1984, one Reagan supporter held up a sign—amid thousands of waving flags—that had a picture of a bomb and the words OUTLAW RUSSIA written on it. Another held up a sign that said, simply, I LIKE YOUR JOKES.

Earlier that same day, according to the *New York Times,* "The President poked fun at himself at a cattle show at the Missouri state fair in Sedalia. Governor Christopher S. Bond presented Mr. Reagan a large prize-winning ham. Holding the ham, Mr. Reagan said he was 'delighted that in view of my former profession you didn't say "sweets to the sweet . . . ham to a ham . . ." ' Here the President and his audience laughed." That was a snappy one, wasn't it? Who else would have made that connection, ham . . . ham?

Sorry. Once I get to quoting the wit of Ronald Reagan, I find it hard to stop. I was going to say something about that sign with the bomb and OUTLAW RUSSIA on it. I was going to say that not many witticisms can be captured in two words and a bomb picture. I'm surprised there hasn't been a T-shirt silk-screen for the president with those very words and that very image. Mr. Reagan has often summarized complex issues by holding up to the cameras T-shirts that have been presented to him. One major-policy T-shirt said, STOP COMMUNISM CENTRAL AMERICA. The president did not himself write this T-shirt, but note the spareness of the prose. Actually, you'd think it would have said, STOP COMMUNISM *IN* CENTRAL AMERICA. I'm not sure what the president was trying to tell us by holding up that T-shirt without the "IN" that you would expect to be there. But *he* must have known. The key to appreciating Reagan, or any other guru, is to feel that the more confusing he is, the more comforting it is just to believe that he's making sense. That's not so hard, is it? It certainly seemed simple enough to an unnamed young woman in the 1984 Reagan campaign film, who stated in all sincerity:

"I think he's just doggone honest. It's remarkable. He's been on television, what have I heard, twenty-six times? Talking to us about what he's doing. He's not doing that for any other reason than to make it real clear. And if anybody has any question about where he's headed, it's their fault. Maybe they don't have a television."

You remember the Russian bombing joke, don't you? It was in August 1984 during a microphone check for his weekly radio broadcast. "My fellow Americans," the president quipped, "I'm pleased to tell you today that I've signed legislation that will outlaw Russia forever. We begin bombing in five minutes."

There is that simplicity: If only we *could* just outlaw Russia.

Forever. It would be a death blow not only to Communism in Central America, but also to the drug problem in this country. Dr. Cory SerVaas illuminated Reagan's fear in an article in *The Saturday Evening Post.* Cory wrote, after chatting with the president at a White House dinner, "He said that the Russians could wipe out our country if they could get a single generation of young people addicted to drugs and marijuana." (The Russians have a few simple ideas of their own. Deadly simple.)

The president realizes, of course, that it is not within his discretion to outlaw Russia, at least not until he gets a couple more appointments to the Supreme Court, but that's where the wit comes in. Not everyone can take a joke, of course. Sober-sides in the media huffed about the "irresponsibility" of the sound-check joke—*when in fact it was the reporters themselves, not the president, who reported it.* "Isn't it funny?" the president pointed out. "If the press had kept their mouth shut, no one would have known I said it." Don't try to get the president confused about what's funny. He knows. You can tell by the look on his face.

And as for joking about nuclear war, hey, come on—it's not the end of the world. The president was joking about bombing *other people.* He wasn't talking about war. On the subject of war, the president has minced no words. He told students at Bowling Green State University that we need better relations with Russia "because peace in America is such an attractive way to live that war is a terrible interruption." Long before this Mikhail-come-lately Gorbachev was coming up with his "disarmament" ploys, President Reagan was working to pacify Russia. As he wrote to a South Dakota man, in a letter reprinted in *Reader's Digest,* ". . . we and the Russian people could be the best of friends if it weren't for the godless tyranny and imperialistic ambitions of their leaders. I said as much in a handwritten note to Brezhnev. His reply was most disappointing."

See, if other people would only face up to their godlessness, we could all live in harmony. But we'll get to the other-people problem in more detail later. First let's look at three presidential observations and see how, through simplicity, Ronald Reagan has redefined the whole meaning of the word *one-liner.*

The budget might be balanced, the president has suggested, "by all of us simply trying to live up to the Ten Commandments and the Golden Rule." How many times have you tried to listen to some commentator make a federal case out of the budget, with all these complicated things about money out and money in? Here the president has cut through all that—in a way that no godless Russian could hope to.

Since there are more businesses in America than there are unemployed people, the unemployment problem would be solved "if a lot of businesses would take a look and see if they could hire just one person." That's so *obvious.* And yet nobody else thought of it.

The homeless could be dealt with if people would just read the newspapers more thoughtfully. At the end of his first news conference on the so-called Iran-contra scandal, the president pointed out that he had read that the city of New York paid $37,000 to support a family in a welfare hotel for a year. "And I wonder why somebody doesn't build them a house for thirty-seven thousand dollars," the president said. (But did somebody do it? No. You know how people are in New York.)

If you can believe it, people in the media have laughed at these suggestions, which are the *wisdom.* These are the same people who *don't* laugh at the wit. I rest my case. These people, who might have a little godlessness problem themselves, ask things like "What if every business in America wants to hire the *same* unemployed person, Donald Regan or somebody?" And "Where and how exactly would you build a house in New York City for thirty-seven thousand dollars?" Well, people laughed at Marie Antoinette, too. But she is the one who's remembered.

Because she had the right line for the right occasion. As does, invariably, the president. On March 3 of this year, he entered the White House pressroom for the first time since more than three months before, when the stuff about the Iran money going to the contras came out. Instead of just being glad to see him, the reporters shouted out, in the snide way that reporters shout out things, "Welcome back." I don't know what I would have said in the president's place. I'd have probably hit one of them. But here's what the president said: "I've never been away."

Pretty hard to think of a comeback to that. And you know why? Because it's simple; but, well, he *was* away—it's complicated too.

Complexity

Those things that win the hearts and minds of great masses of Americans—wrestling, television evangelists, chain letters—are all things that *seem* simple, but we know we should not be too quick to understand them. For instance, take a teenage holy man who, because he is God, can speak any language, yet chooses to communicate in broken English. Try to fathom that by mere intellect alone! So too with the wit and wisdom of Ronald Reagan.

"Yes, there has been an increase in poverty, but it is a lower rate of increase than it was in the preceding years before we got here. It has begun to decline, but it is still going up."

I can see it—bobbing, hovering, almost like a UFO . . . but wait! You don't know how it soars above statistics. If you believe in statistics, the rate of increase of the number of Americans living in poverty has been twice as high during the Reagan years as during the Carter years. So what the president is saying is *more complex* than statistics. And yet its message is so clear: If you were thinking of joining the disadvantaged, think twice.

"Over something less than one hundred documents have some part in what's going on now," the president said, dodging a question about the so-called scandal in the Environmental Protection Administration in 1983. He cleared up that "scandal," didn't he? In over something less than fourteen words, he beautifully captured what a drag it is to keep up with things.

This is how the president dealt with accusations that his administration had knowingly disseminated "disinformation" about plans to take even firmer measures against Colonel Qaddafi than blowing up his daughter, which we had already done:

"Our position—this was wrong and false—our position has been one of which, after we took the action we felt we had to take, and I still believe was the correct thing to do, our position has been one in which we would just as soon have Mr. Qaddafi go to bed every night wondering what we might do."

There is the genius of Ronald Reagan. He lets them all wonder—the press, the Congress, the daughters of those who would foster violence, the Russians, the Democrats. All of whom come under one heading:

Other People

In 1968, Ronald Reagan spoke to Texas conservatives who were thinking of backing him instead of Richard Nixon for the Republican presidential nomination. "I'd be the most enthusiastic, energetic, and active campaigner you've ever seen." Reagan promised. "Because *they* have got to *go.*"

Yes! They! Ronald Reagan has put his finger on exactly who is causing all our problems: *them out there.*

He doesn't always name them, but we know he didn't mean himself, and we knew he didn't mean us, when he said on TV early this year, "I'm not going to tell falsehoods to the American people. I'll leave that to others."

"When other people were burning our flag," he told a picnic crowd in Decatur, Alabama, "you were waving it." (Probably not the best way to put it out.) He finished his speech by saying,

"And I don't know if a president has ever thanked you for that."
Well, no! What other president would take time out from his
glamorous schedule to thank people in Alabama for getting down
to the hard work of waving the flag?

He is *interested* in other people. When he returned from
his first trip to South America, he told us, "Well, I learned a
lot. . . . You'd be surprised. They're all individual countries."

But he knows they aren't him or us. "This whole thing boils
down to a great irresponsibility on the part of the press," he said
with regard to the so-called Iran-contra scandal. The press is
always other people. And, of course, the Democrats, whose
great society is to blame for everything wrong domestically. The
Republican party, he points out, is becoming America's party.
Who needs a party of the others? In this country, that is. There
is one in Russia, of course. In Russia, they have no word for
"freedom," the president tells us; and even though in Russia
they do have a word for "freedom," we know what he means.

Americans, even if they aren't Democrats or reporters, can
become others if they don't watch out. One of the president's
biggest laughs came when he proposed that protesting
farmers—instead of grain—be exported to Russia. Congress, as
a whole, is already others. After addressing the staff of NASA,
the president took time out from his busy day to appear at a
photo opportunity and said, "I just got back from outer space,
too—Capitol Hill."

Which brings up probably the most cosmic idea the president
has come up with. Chatting with Gorbachev, he mentioned (he
confided to us later) that the two leaders would find their nego-
tiations easier "if suddenly there was a threat to this world from
some other species from another planet outside the universe.
We would forget all the little differences that we have between
our countries, and we would find out once and for all that we
really are all human beings on this earth together."

Wouldn't that be great? Invasion by a whole new species.
If that didn't bring the Russians back to God, and stimulate

both of our economies and not so incidentally make a heck of a movie . . .

I'm reminded of what the president said when people accused his wife, Nancy, of being too powerful. (She can't possibly be *too* powerful, of course, because she is not one of the others. The president himself is not too powerful by his own account: "They tell me I'm the most powerful man in the world. I don't believe that. Over there in the White House someplace, there's a fellow that puts a piece of paper on my desk every day that tells me what I'm going to be doing every fifteen minutes. He's the most powerful man in the world." What if *he* became one of the others? Never happen, not with Ronald Reagan in charge.)

What the president said when people accused Nancy of being too powerful is something that applies not only to people who doubt the president's vision of world peace through outer-space invasion. It applies to *all* those other people, of whom there have been so many over the last six years. Here is what he said. And I hope all those other people take it to heart: "A lot of people ought to be ashamed of themselves."

THE NEW AVARICE

. . . . . .

With the old avarice, didn't everybody feel *logy*? It was all about, like, physically having your own money. Literally owning whole things. People would say, "This is our home, free and clear. And we've got thirty thousand socked away." Can you imagine that? Sitting on all that raw equity, and loving it?

The new avarice is *float*. Floating on how much more you owe than you're worth. Your own money, you've got to worry about. Other people's money, *they've* got to worry about. While you feel it lift you.

What they had back in literature was the old avarice. Avarice is this guy in *The Faerie Queene* riding on a camel with—yuck—ingots.

> And thread-bare cote, and cobled shoes he ware,
> Ne scarce good morsell all his life did tast.

"Cobled" meant "patched up." Who gets shoes cobled today? *Lease* shoes is what I do. The last cobler in my neighborhood was replaced by a Brazilian-Malaysian-Philippine produce stand, which is hot since it started taking plastic, but I hear the whole block is being leveled for a skyscraper-mall complex. Good thing I didn't get into exotic-fruit futures—not that carambola and ajicahuc are all that exotic anymore.

The old avarice thought leverage was what it took to hoist your stuff onto the camel. The guy on the camel did do a little finance:

Accursèd usurie was all his trade.

But who wants to be a usurer anymore? Look where it's gotten the banks. The key is to be the usuree. As a nation, we're being usured by foreign creditors and future generations for this $2 trillion (and strong dollars, too, not wimp dollars) we owe. Hey, let 'em squeeze us. Just squooshes us up higher.

How high? I'll tell you how high. Star Wars high. I can't believe these people talking about how Star Wars will still let missiles get in. What the hell. We're a nation of open arms. What Star Wars is mainly going to do is let *money* get in. We're a debtor nation, right? You don't think foreign creditors and future generations are going to spend a little to protect their investment? Nobody's even started thinking about outer space as real estate yet. It's *perfect* real estate. It keeps going up forever, and you don't have to maintain it. I don't know why you couldn't depreciate it. But, okay, say while we're developing outer space a couple of missiles do get through, do a little damage. You don't think foreign creditors and future generations are going to lay a little Marshall Plan on us?

And we *party*. Throw a concert:

We owe the world.
We owe the children.

And this is a sin? If it is, I don't blame us. We cut a deal. If foreign creditors and future generations of Americans don't like it, let them do business somewhere else. What are they going to do, foreclose? How many lawyers have *they* got?

One thing I would like to see. A new amendment to the Constitution. I would like to see every American who qualifies (who flies at least business class) be entitled to life, liberty, the pursuit of happiness, and a golden parachute.

BOREDOM NOW

*(This is something I wrote back in the Reagan
administration at the behest of* Playboy, *whose
editors to this day have not printed it. I can't
say I blame them. But I have worked on it
and pared it down and updated it a bit and
punched it up some for this occasion and,
snore . . .)*

What a lush period we live in! Every week sees the
dawning of new megapersonalities—impossibly rich, androgynous, muscled, coiffed, phosphorescent, surly. It's as hard to
stay abreast of the names on everyone's lips as it is to keep track
of the ever-advancing techniques of resurrection surgery that,
by and by, will make it old-fashioned for anyone to die except
from exploding pectorals or absentmindedness while driving
$90,000 sports cars on the moon.

We can now drowse in our own parlors while watching
videotapes—rented legally at $2 a day—in which cheerleaders,
midgets, snakes, passing mailmen, and uncle-niece combos go at
it (lifting their legs to make sure we can see) in variations not
even speculated upon, even by the dirtiest boys, even out behind the barn, when I was a lad.

It is now possible, through pluck and luck, to make, oh,
$19,846,000 a year. And to pick up seventy-four different TV
channels. There is a drug called ecstasy that apparently enables
you to achieve nirvana and then brush yourself off and go practice corporate law. Today you can do math on a calculator the
size of a playing card, take over a company with "junk bonds,"
splash on a fragrance called Obsession (just right for those
moments when you find yourself entangled in several perfectly
formed limbs), and carry a telephone to the beach.

And what does it all lead to?

Boredom.

Ho-hum, you may say.

See, you've got it, too. According to the experts, it's rampant. You can get bored, the experts say, from too much stimulation as well as from too little. (Or from television, which provides both at once.) And boredom can lead to depression, addiction, hallucinations, or the total destruction of the planet.

Right, right. Total D. of the P. You've heard that one before.

Have you got a case of boredom! It's the latest hot disease. Says Estelle Ramey, professor of physiology and biophysics at Georgetown University, "It's not considered a disease, but it *is* one, because it causes all kinds of problems. . . . When you look at society, a lot of what has happened, including wars, has been to escape from boredom."

See. War. And you know what that leads to these days. Total . . .

And you just shrug, don't you?

Okay, how about this: total destruction of the planet, except (by some quirk of fate) you, a patch of swamp, and all the world's insects and alligators. And the Joint Chiefs of Staff. Who are perched on the last five tree limbs in existence, clutching every tube of Bug-Off left in creation and—just to keep themselves occupied—yelling militaristic things at you (things that make your blood boil, because you were honorably excused from military service in 1971 on grounds of schizophrenia and sensitivity to others):

"Pull in your gut!"

"Shape up or ship out!"

"*Puh*-raaaaaade . . . *hrest*!

"I don't know, but I been told/Eskimo pussy is mighty cold."

And—wait a minute—it's not just you down there in the mud but also . . . Tina Turner! And she's singing! And she's wearing this little *wisp* of a . . . And she *needs* you!

And wait a minute! The Joint Chiefs aren't just being predictably commanding. They've gone crazy! They are beginning to shout escalating confessions:

"I stole an epaulet once!"

"I told a dying man he was goofing off!"

"I was the one who advised the president to go ahead and push the button! Just to see what he would do!"

"No! No! It was me! And I just did it off the top of my head!"

"No, you didn't—I did!"

And Tina is singing . . . deeply . . . calling to you . . . You always wished you could have known her before Ike. . . .

And here come five, six, seven pissed-off, power-mad alligators—*glowing in the dark.*

The terrible thing is, you could get bored with all *that.* Because that would fall into the category of sensory overload, which experts say can cause psychological numbing, just as sensory deprivation can. Some people get bored with eating mescaline and scaling a sheer rock face and running through the positions of the *Kama Sutra* (boredom has all the same letters as bedroom) day in and day out. Other people get bored with waiting for their children to call.

Boring as what you are reading undeniably is, it is a lot less boring than a book called *What to Do When You're Bored and Blue,* by Sam Keen, Ph. D. Dr. Keen believes that boredom is an epidemic, "our number-one social disease." He prescribes "The Whole-Some Life: Beyond Boredom."

I know; it's boring that his name is Keen. I, too, would rather his name were Blah. Bobby Blue Blah, the almost-comatose balladeer:

> *Well, I can get more bored on Saturday night*
> *Than you after lunch on Wedne-*
> *Sday. Boring, boring, out-a-sight,*
> *Till I come out the other end.*

As a matter of fact, that is pretty close to something that Keen recommends: *Go with* boredom, he suggests. Listen to what it has to tell you. Maybe the people who aren't bored today are the ones who don't understand the situation. At a time like this, when we've just had eight years of geriatric space-cadet presidency and the prevailing mood is narrow-minded profligacy, maybe it is more commendable to be bored than . . .

Listen, this is boring me just as much as it is you. Yes it is, too. Probably more. I can be more bored *and/or* boring than the average reader the slowest day he or she ever had. Think. Picture yourself being so bored and/or boring that *flies* take no interest in you, and you wish they would. I can be more bored and/or boring than that. I *have been* so boring people not only slept but gratefully died. I *have been* so bored moss grew on my jowls. And vow'ls. Listen, talk about vowels, one time I pronounced an *a* so long that I got so tired of it in the middle that I went off to the store and bought cigarettes waiting for myself to finish. *And neither I nor anyone in my family smoked. We never have. We just never have seen the value of it.* How about a little etymology?

You know what the derivation of the word *boredom* is? If you do, you're smarter than the *Oxford English Dictionary*, which says, "If related at all to [the verb *bore,* to drill holes], the connection must be indirect; possibly there is an allusion to some now-forgotten anecdote."

Let's see. Guy is sitting against a wall, somebody's drilling a hole from the other side, drill goes through the wall and into the guy's aorta, the life drains out of him. And he was just getting ready to get up and do something, too.

"What's wrong with Gareth, there?"

"Got bored."

Breasts . . . soft . . . bare . . . one quivering drop of . . .

I of course got far too bored with Keen's book to get very far into it, but I read enough to find out this: If you really want to get beyond your tired, muddled, frenzied apathy, you have to ask yourself, "What do I really want?"

But what if you do ask yourself that question and yourself says in reply, "If you have to ask, you'll never know"?

Within the next few years, I daresay, you'll be able to tell yourself to take a hike. Designer selves will be available, and even if you find *them* boring and don't want to fight the crowds at Selves R Us, you can order from a Selves in the Rough catalog—irregular imports. A self from Mozambique: fourteen years old, stone hungry, never tasted ice cream. You might even be tempted by the fanatic Lebanese. That would keep you hopping. Or a Thai self might appeal. Or how about a Haitian? Who'd be bored with voodoo down inside?

The trouble is that those selves will *all* look good in the catalog. How will you choose? You'll try several and come down with self overload.

What can save us? Maybe a particularly diverting depression will come along and boredom as we know it will go out of style. In the meantime, we can aspire to be *good* and bored.

Along those lines, I have one concrete proposal. It's not very eighties, but here it is.

One day when I was a little kid, I didn't have anything available to me except 1,486 toys, books, pets, snacks, catchable reptiles, and climbable trees. So I said to my mother, "What can I do? I don't have anything to do."

"Well," she replied, "you can help me finish waxing these floors and then go with me to the home and be sweet to Miss Maybelle while I wash her hair, poor old soul, and then . . ."

I did not want any part of waxing floors. And I did not want to be sweet to Miss Maybelle at the home, either. She was about ninety years old, she was skin and bones, she didn't have any family, she lay flat on her back all day long wishing someone would come visit her so she could ask again and again where she was, she loved having her hair washed, and she scared the bejesus out of me.

So I ran along and played vigilante. I had seen a movie about good-guy vigilantes that hadn't scared me at all. I tied a handkerchief over my lower face and ran around shooting caps, out-outlawing the outlaws. That kept me occupied for a while.

These days, however, I don't think vigilantism is the answer. Here's what I think: bored as you may be, you aren't as bored as Miss Maybelle was. Go find some poor old soul and be sweet to her.

NEWS FOR THE
LISTENING IMPAIRED

. . . .

The literary neurologist Oliver Sacks, whose *The Man Who Mistook His Wife for a Hat* is the best book of nonfiction I have read since Evan S. Connell's about Custer's Last Stand, has written a piece for *The New York Review of Books* titled "Mysteries of the Deaf," which has suggested to me a new avenue toward world harmony.

In his books Sacks explores eerie disorders of the nervous system (such as the brain damage that caused a pianist, who was lucid in most ways, to take hold of his wife's head and try to set it atop his own) and finds engrossingly humane order in the adjustments that sufferers have made. In this new essay he tells what he learned when he began to read about deafness and the manual sign language, called Sign, that the deaf use eloquently.

Sack's primary focus is on how best to liberate the deaf, who for centuries were dismissed as "dumb" (or, more elegantly, "sentient statues") and denied citizenship. Even in recent history they have been frustrated by educators' outrageous insistence that they eschew signing and speak only orally. Deaf children, Sacks writes, "show an immediate and powerful disposition to sign. This is most apparent in the deaf children of deaf parents using sign language, who make their first signs when they are about six months old and have considerable sign-fluency by the age of fifteen months. This is intriguingly earlier than the 'normal' acquisition of speech, suggesting that our linguistic development is, so to speak, retarded by speech, by the complexity of neuromuscular control required. If we are to communicate with babies, we may find that the way to do so is with Sign."

Well. My children have never had hearing problems, but if they were babies I would go learn sign language right now and teach it to them. (My daughter knows it, in fact, but she learned it at nineteen, in a course at Stanford.) "There is no evidence that signing inhibits the acquisition of speech," Sacks says. "Indeed the reverse is probably so."

So why not start striking up dialogues with babies, deaf or not, as early as possible? And if a great many parents started doing that, and their babies began signing among themselves in play group; if Sign caught on among infants in the nineties the way rock-and-roll did among teenagers in the fifties . . . wouldn't it begin to change, and why not to enhance, the way *most* people converse? (My post-Elvis teenage children and their peers don't read as eagerly as I did at their age, but they do talk among themselves more sensibly, less defensively, more fluently and helpfully, than my peers and I did until we were, oh, thirty.) And wouldn't video spread it around the world? Rock stars might even sign while they sing and dance.

One of the books Sacks read about deafness was *Everyone Here Spoke Sign Language: Hereditary Deafness on Martha's Vineyard,* by Nora Ellen Groce. For 250 years (the last local "deaf mute" died in 1952) hereditary deafness was so wide-spread on that Massachusetts island that everyone mastered Sign, and even after the deafness genes had all receded, older residents with good hearing held on to the language, because it came naturally to them and it could say things speech couldn't. Sacks was moved to visit the Vineyard himself. He found a talkative ninety-year-old woman whose fingers moved when she thought and even when she dreamed. Sign, Sacks concludes, is "a fundamental language of the brain."

That doesn't make it a panacea, Lord knows. But what if— even given all the territorial problems—what if Custer and the Sioux had been speaking the same sign language since they were six months old?

GATHER ROUND, COLLEGIANS

Generally my advice to young people is, Don't listen to advice. I say that not only because it is something young people will listen to. I say it also because questionable advice ("Hey, organic chemistry will take care of itself") is always so much more appealing than sound advice ("Worry about everything").

But this year I am a sophomore parent. That is, my daughter Ennis is a sophomore at Stanford. That is, I believe she is. Since Stanford's policy is not to send grades, comportment ratings, or even bills, as such, to parents, her only connection with the university may be that she has a room, a mailing address, and a number of college-age-looking friends there. Of these things I have personal knowledge. (One of the friends, Chuck Gerardo, a gymnast, feels that he has invented a dance step called the Goober, which entails moving exactly counter to the beat. In point of fact I stumbled upon a subtler and rather more complex version of that step myself, quite a few years ago, and by now it has become more or less second nature—give or take a half-sh'boom—to me. You young people today aren't necessarily the first people in history to be hup. Hep.) And every so often I receive word from Ennis that she has made five more A-pluses and needs another $47,000 for gasoline, incidentals, and felt-tip pens. (We didn't have felt-tips in my day. We improvised: Q-tips and our own blood. We parents want to spare you all that—in fact, *don't bleed.*)

So I know, as surely as I know most things, that I am a sophomore parent. And it may be that there is no one who knows more about anything, aside from a sophomore student about life outside college, than a sophomore parent about life inside college. It may also be that I am being incredibly unassuming and gracious, as parents are, as you will realize when you are parents.

So if you would just stop darting your eyes around for one moment, please.

• Eat pizza. (See, you thought I was going to come down hard. Not at all. Parents do not come down nearly as hard as they have every right to, because parents came *up* hard, and are tired.) Chuck Noll, the head coach of the Pittsburgh Steelers, once told me that pizza contains every element of the human body. For a while this put me off pizza. But the Steelers won the Super Bowl that year, so Noll must have been right: There is no more perfect food. Even *gigot de français* (leg of Frenchman), say, does not contain *every* element of the human body. I don't think. You could check me on that, with your School of Medicine. Or Romance Languages. Oh, the banquet of knowledge that is spread out before you.

• Learn a trade. Even if it is something so highly technical that of course it makes us very proud of you, but perhaps is not the most considerate field you could have gone into, since how can we tell whether you are doing it right? Every moment that you aren't learning a trade, worry about why you aren't. This is known as pure thought. Or "unadulterated" thought, so called because adults cannot afford to indulge in it. By *trade* I mean something that will support aging parents, suitably, before you know it.

• Save mailing tubes. Those cardboard tubes. I tried to buy one recently, in which to mail someone something, and looked all over everywhere. I could have bought an expensive fancy plastic art-supply deal with caps on the ends, suitable for shipping a Caravaggio to the Vatican, but I didn't want that. I wanted just a regular cardboard tube, the kind you receive in the mail with something non-invaluable rolled up in it. I could not buy one for love or money. I had to learn this the hard way. You don't.

• Finish up in four years. Maximum. Every extra day after four years means another three months off your parents' lives. There has been a study on this. By a university. Whose bursar suppressed the findings.

• Don't keep small, gnawing pets, such as hamsters, in your room. Hamsters get loose and eat money. This is why college costs so much. *Why does college cost so much?* Oh, you want to change the subject! You want to know how my generation has managed to run up a $2,000,000,000,000 debt. Well, how else can we send you through college in 100 percent natural-fiber clothes? The natural-fiber money ran out! I'll tell you this: My college roommate insisted on keeping a hamster, and one night it got into my wallet and ate everything. It was a valuable lesson. There are some things we can't control. *But we can do without insidious little animals out there in the darkness gnawing.*

• Cling to eternal verities. This is all recent, you know, all these post-hypen-you-name-it-isms. Post-modernism, post-vandalism, whatever. We didn't have any of them in my day, and we didn't exactly come to town on a load of rutabagas. Mark my words: These things will blow over.

• So will everything else. Except parents. Who will just get pitiful and die. But you let us worry about that. You just worry about how bad you are going to feel—too late.

• If some fad like riding five to a motorcycle backward or watching insect-monster movies for seventy-two hours straight while wearing nothing but feelers arises, hey, you're only young once. But think what it will do to your parents. They are only going to be middle-aged once, which is all they have left, and perhaps not for long. Call your parents. Talk to them—*about something else*—until the urge passes.

• On the other hand, what makes you feel the need to take sixteen courses in accounting? We're sending you to college so you can learn everything there is to know about the bottom line? You want to know about the bottom line? Call your parents.

• *Drugs.* Young people don't need to get high. Young people are already, *qua* young people, higher than they will ever be again, even tomorrow. Wait until you are seventy. There is no one more tickled with himself or herself than a seventy-year-old college graduate who *feels* seventy but who has not yet developed a tolerance for killer Nepalese mushrooms.

• *Politics.* I fully realize that the point of collegiate political activity is to make all the blood drain out of your parents' faces. Fine. Fair enough. But if anything involving heavy explosives ever comes back in style, remember that you will be alumni soon. For every $100,000 in damage done to campus property, you may count on receiving two dozen solicitations to contribute to the building fund. In demolitions, as in economics, there is no such thing as a free boom. On the other hand, before you plunge headlong into your Campus Young Arch-Reactionary Club, stop and think. Shouldn't *some* gratifications be deferred until you can no longer enjoy anything else?

• *Plagiarism.* This above all, to thine own self be true.

• *Extramarital relations.* Never marry your relatives. See? Parents can laugh about these things. As long as we are sure your heads are on straight. Once we realize that they aren't, we can never laugh again.

• Excuse me. Will you please stop doing that with your corneas when I am talking to you? Yes, your corneas. You know what I mean.

• Yes, you do.

• And don't expect to remember any of this, unless you write it all down. Right now. The older you get, the less you remember, even tomorrow.

• Any of what?

ITALIAN WASN'T LEARNED IN A DAY

*P*er favore, ci riservi un tavolo per due per le due."

This was me speaking! Reserving a table for two for two o'clock at Sabatini I, a restaurant in Rome. Over the Italian telephone, coolly. Italian wouldn't melt in my mouth. And then the man who had answered the phone said, in his native tongue (my translation):

"Men?"

Why would he ask that? As a matter of fact, my twosome was mixed. What business of his was it whether . . . And what made him think he ought to check? Was it something I said? My thoughts sped like wildfire. . . .

No, that's *spread* like wildfire, isn't it? The deeper I get into Italian, the more my English suffers. My thoughts sped, like . . . something fast, back over what I had said.

Un tavolo. I knew that was right. Unless—was there some word that sounded a lot like *tavolo* that had nonheterosexual connotations? And what if there was? What was the securely but uninvidiously straight response here, in Italian? How would I know? I'd had only five and a quarter hours of Italian, not counting lunch. And lunch had not been all that Italian because it was included in the $387.06 I'd paid for a one-day crash course in Italian at Berlitz in midtown Manhattan, and all the Italian restaurants around there were expensive, so my instructor and I had eaten at La Bonne Soupe.

But my studies lay five days in the past. Now I was in Rome, on the firing line, and . . . wait. How could you conduct any sort of restaurant business by telephone if there was a word with nonheterosexual connotations that sounded like the word for "table"?

Maybe the problem lay in the *dues.* (If my mastery of the language were greater, I sensed quickly, I might be able to make a joke about having paid my *dues,* but I had neither time nor Italian enough for that now.) Was it possible I had given the impression that I was reserving a table for two people named Dewey and Dewey, the latter of them referred to for some reason as *the* Dewey?

No. Wait. The word for "man" in Italian was *uomo* (no connotations), the plural was *uomini.* What the man taking reservations had said was *"Signori?"* Which meant "Gentlemen?"

What he really wanted to know, then, was whether Dewey and the Dewey were of the right class. The nerve! (*Il nervo!*) Perhaps my Italian was not on a par with that of some vestigial patrician whose ancestors had scattered like rabbits (*conigli*) at the first hint of Visigoths, but where did this guy get off . . . ?

"Americano?" he said then.

Oh ho, I thought to myself (in English, because I'd had only the one day's immersion in Italian). Restaurants in Rome had a quota on Americans named Dewey. I was angry—but how to express it?

"Si . . ." I said, temporizing, sticking to basic vocabulary, struggling to put some kind of spin on the word that would sound like . . . some kind of spin.

Then he said a thing that hurt my feelings. "Are you talking?" he said. In English.

And then, as I groped for a suitably stiff reply to this impertinent question, something else hit me. What he must have said to begin with was not *"Signori?"* but *"Signore . . . ?"* as in

"Mister . . . ?" He must simply have wanted to know what my last name was so he could book the reservation. Was it too late to answer that question now? Unfortunately, my name—four consonants surrounding one sluggish, questionable vowel sound—does not sound like anything at all in Italian.

I decided to deal with the most recent question. *"Si . . ."* I said. Fighting for time.

Then it occurred to me that perhaps *"Signore?"* had just meant "Sir?" But I couldn't pause to mull that over because it would require several more split seconds of silence and I had just said yes, I was talking.

". . . in inglese?" he asked. Which means, "in English?"

"No," I said, in Italian. But how do you say "I am speaking in Italian" in Italian? *Io parlo italiano* means "I speak Italian," which wasn't strictly true, as I had had only the seven lessons plus lunch.

"In English or Italian, are you talking or are you not talking? Come on man, wake up," he said. In English. I won't be spoken to like that. Not in my own first language. I hung up.

"Are you talking?" indeed! Easy for him to talk. He is a person who answers the telephone in Italian for a living. Whereas I . . .

When my one-day course at Berlitz began, I couldn't speak more than a handful of words in Italian. When it ended, I couldn't speak more than a handful of words in English, either.

But that was fatigue. A person would feel that way after being immersed all day in anything—water, for instance. I took seven forty-five minute classes, and French lunch, in Italian. And I got to where I was speaking up to three sentences at a stretch! If you count *"No"* as a sentence. For example: *"Sono io la signora Dussi? No. Io sono il signore Blount."*

I spent a whole day speaking scarcely a word of English, except *sotto voce.* (The walls—*le pareti*—had ears. My several instructors would point to the walls and whisper, "They are listening." That is, the school's management was monitoring, making sure we were confining ourselves to Italian. Confining ourselves! To the least pinched, at least *sentimento*-wise, of tongues!)

There my instructors and I were, tearing off great chunks of Italian, all about doors and doctors and hats (*cappelli*). Pictures were held up. Fingers were pointed. Hand gestures were made. Verbs and conjunctions were rendered inferable. (*E* is "and," and *è* is "is.") And at one point Signora Dussi—the only one of my teachers whose name I got entirely straight—said to me, "*Bravissimo!*"

Which means "Bravo very much."

Let me say that I majored in English for four years of college and one of graduate school. And in that entire time no teacher ever said to me, "*Bravissimo!*" Of course I never came up with anything in English that sounded as good as this:

"*L'Arno non è una strada e non è una città.*"

Which is pronounced:

"Larno known eh oona strada ay known eh oona cheetah."

And which means: "The Arno is not a street and is not a city."

And which is the closest I can come, in Italian, to "I know a little place called diddy-wah-diddy. It ain't no town and it ain't no city."

Imagine my being able to come that close to something that hip in Italian! I can even tell you what the Arno is. *È un lungo fiume.*

What a fine language Italian is in many ways. As I understand it, every little syllable is pronounced, wholeheartedly. Which I think is something the French ought to look into. The French, if you ask me, take undue advantage of the fact that so much of their language amounts to elaborate but probably indistinguishable variations on *ong.* I took French in high school and college, but in my experience if you try to speak it to a Frenchman whom you are not paying anything or whom you have already paid, he will look at you as if you are not speaking anything at all.

Whereas my day's worth of Berlitz Italian, supplemented by a phrase book, enabled me to ask a Roman waiter, "*Perchè non ci sono carciofi?"* And although he was already pocketing the tip, and I am not at all sure the *ci* was in the right place, he answered at some length and I could sort of follow him. There were no artichokes because the weather was not right, there had not been enough water. From what I gather, he was even telling the truth. An Italian, speaking to me with perfect candor in Italian.

"Grazie," I said, and I meant it.

On the other hand, as we have seen, there was my experience with the man who answered the phone at Sabatini I. So I am not going to fall head over heels into Italian.

I have a pretty good thing going with American English. It keeps food in my mouth. Is that right? That can't be right. It keeps food on the table. That doesn't seem quite right either. But when it comes to American English, I am constantly *aware* that I never quite know what I am saying.

One night in Rome, in the American bar of the Hotel de la Ville, I spoke, in English, with a Japanese businessman about America. He was from Hiroshima, but he said he didn't hold that against me. He said in fact he was glad that Americans had occupied Japan because his people had learned much from our culture. However, he said, there was one thing about Americans . . . He searched for an example.

A colleague of his, he said, had been in America. Had penetrated so far as Ohio. And there, in a private home, this colleague "was served a sandwich of penis butter. Penis butter? Penis butter. I think it is an example of Protestantism and capitalism."

"Ah," I said. I looked at him, and nodded. And I thought to myself (in English): I have been speaking Italian. And people have been looking at me, and nodding.

TV *GONE BLANK FOR GOOD*

· · · · · ·

It just got to be so hard. The people in the industry threw up their hands. And all the big TV execs returned home, weary and suddenly limoless, to children who cried, "Do something! None of our sets are working!"

"It's not the sets," the execs all said. "It's television. We have stopped putting it out. Television is over."

"It can't be over!" cried the children (some of whom were in their forties). "It's still light out! It's time for *Wheel of Family Feud!*"

"Over," said the execs. "There's not going to be any more TV."

"Why?" cried the shocked and uncomprehending children, who preferred to watch the Huxtables sort things out.

"It just got to be so hard," said the execs. "It's easy for you. All you have to do is push a button and there, bingo, is a shot of anything in the world. But if you had to arrange for that shot to appear, and the next shot, and the next and the next . . ." The execs sighed. It had become too hard to explain, even.

For so long, the television audience—that is to say, humanity—had taken the filling of all those time slots for granted. But no second of television is achieved without staggering commitments of time, imagination, legal opinions, yelling, and money.

And the money tightened up, and the competition grew, and the fun went out of it. It was like frantically putting food on the table constantly, constantly, for people who just sucked it up and belched and opened their mouths for more—and were picky, to boot. (Another thing that hit the industry hard was when Vanna White, having gotten a taste of authorship, dropped out of television and went full-time into belles-lettres.)

So the people who gave us TV stopped giving. And a glumness fell over the land.

Nothing ever quite came out right anymore. No overwhelming problem was ever resolved in an hour's time, much less thirty minutes. A syndrome set in; no one ever quite got the name of it straight because there were no morning-show doctors to get it through our heads, but it involved restlessness, dissatisfaction, a tendency not be comfortable any longer at home. People glared at each other and looked away, not satisfied. Each other's faces weren't as gratifying as the ones on *Falcon Crest.*

No one came into people's homes except other people—who just sort of sat there, unbolstered by the highly developed levels of laughter, welcome, music, and explicability that people had become used to. Also people lost their pride in, their special love of, goods and services. Margarine was just margarine. It no longer danced and sang.

Some foresaw that the leaders of the new society would be those who had scorned television, or whose parents had forbidden them to watch it, when it was available. But this did not turn out to be true. The new society was overwhelmingly one of nostalgia for TV. People who did not appreciate what was lost were like prewar people in a postwar age.

There were still VCRs, of course, but that wasn't the same. VCRs placed such an onus on the viewer. You had to go out and select tapes, and if there were boring stretches you could always fastforward through them. Real television had its own rhythms and authority, like the weather. It had always been there, continually underway, going about its business like a subterranean river. People couldn't believe that they couldn't tune in anymore. They tried, but TV had dried up. Conservation groups arose, but it was too late. There was no more TV to conserve.

Some marriages were destroyed, some were strengthened. Politics got less misleading in some ways, more in others. People who had been incited to violence by television committed less violence, but they were more or less balanced out by those who were incited to violence by the lack of television.

Having an American president with a large birthmark on his forehead was strange. It would have been unthinkable in the TV days. But it was not so much the broad sociological and political shifts that made people feel weird After Television. It was a more personal thing. A sense of loss. Everyone, it seemed, had a different small memory.

For Mary, it was Ted Koppel being a bit *too* firm with a Russian, in a subtly self-sacrificing way that made her see not only beyond the Russian but even a bit beyond Ted, into his vulnerability.

For John, it was Cybill Shepherd winking—not live, of course, but not in a rerun, either. Winking downright—okay, it was Cybill Shepherd playing the role of Maddie winking at the audience, but still . . . Winking downright provocatively. At John.

For little Toby and little Meryl, it was Bill Murray, on *Late Night with David Letterman,* dragging a majorette and two midgets from the wings and piling them, one on top of the other (the majorette first), on the chair next to David—midget on midget on majorette—just to reveal the immense possibilities of life to kids who could stay up late enough to catch Letterman.

Everyone had a different small, unshakable memory. A memory of a time when a medium—no, more than a medium. A memory of a time when a great *supernatural tide,* mightier than the Mississippi, was channeled into everyone's home. An endless tide of imagery—which seemed, every now and then, so fleetingly we almost missed it, actually to be showing us something.

TV *NEWS NEVER GETS WET*

. . . . .

Sounds like a wrestling tag team (bad guys): Van Gordon "Hoity-Toity" Sauter and Creed "Priest of Satan" Black. But no. They are not on the same side.

Van Gordon Sauter is in *television* news. Executive vice-president in charge of news for CBS. He says newspaper reporters are "insipid," "ill-informed," and "ignorant." (Presumably, they don't watch CBS News.)

Creed Black is in *newspaper* news. Chairman and publisher of the *Lexington Herald-Leader* in Kentucky. He says, "What the networks call 'news' is, in fact, a mixture of analysis, opinion, and speculation." (He neglects to mention pictures.)

Both these men are in the business of telling the truth. So they both must be right. But if you ask me, that doesn't mean we should stop viewing and reading news. Or even that we should stop paying attention to news executives altogether.

What we should do, I think, is accept, once and for all, that television and newspaper news are two different things. Here are the essential distinctions:

Television news never killed a dog. Certainly not Barbara Bain's. According to newspaper accounts (I never saw anything about this on television, oddly enough), Bain threatened to sue the *Los Angeles Times* recently, alleging that a rolled-up copy of that gravid publication, possibly tossed by a paperboy, struck and killed her dog on her Beverly Hills lawn. I don't know whether malice has been established as a factor, but perhaps in the case of a life-styles-of-the-rich-and-famous canine it could be assumed.

Television news never gets wet. If there is anything that no one, at any point on the political spectrum, can stand, it is a wet newspaper. You get all caught up in a page-one story about the tornado that came down and picked up an entire church-wedding-in-progress and plunged it, after a while, into Lake Erie: "Whooo," the sole survivor (the groom's Uncle Barry) is quoted as saying. "It was a mess. I lost every last one of my relatives and my fig-

You notice that I do not close the quotation. That is because it never closes. "See p. 33," says a note at the bottom of the column. When you attempt to reach p. 33 you find yourself with an armload of strips and wads and giblets of sodden paper. Uncle Barry's figleaf? Uncle Barry's figure skates? You never find out. Because when you rush to the nearest newsstand after a dry copy of the paper, the Late Blue Streak edition is already out and its lead headline is "Twister Wedding Survivor Admits Hoax." The accompanying story is rife with new developments, none of which entail any words beginning with "fig."

Newspaper news never shares its technical problems with us. Television news does. The anchorperson leads into the big story about a liberal cabal's attempt to buy controlling interest in the Moral Majority so as to replace the Rev. Jerry Falwell with the Rev. William Sloane Coffin. "More on that now from Burns Wiglift in the nation's capital." And then the anchorperson sits there for several precious moments, looking us—vacantly—right in the eye. And then as if by magic the anchorperson is supplanted by a sort of test pattern and a small, almost subliminal sound like *fbweep*. And then the anchorperson reappears and says, "I'm afraid we are having technical problems with the remote feed." And we understand.

You can't think while watching the television news. Unless you

are willing to be left behind. A person who is "buried in his newspaper" can resurrect himself, ponder, and then go back down for more, which is still there waiting for him. If the same person allows his mind to take its own course during a thought-provoking news segment on world hunger, the next thing he knows he is inside a washing machine, where shorts and socks with faces on them are dancing and singing a whitener's praises.

You can skim right over certain parts of a newspaper. The ads, for instance. Persons who want newspapers to survive, however, resist the temptation.

You can't think, except in a sort of catch-as-catch-can fashion, while being interviewed on television. This, I believe, has a certain effect on television news. As one who has been interviewed on television, I can tell you that when someone asks me, "How did you go about writing your new major novel?" I respond crisply, "The characters came to me during breakfast, and it took me a while to get them unscrambled"—*even though I have in fact never written a major novel.* Or any novel at all. If a television interviewer wants to assume that I have written a major novel, well:

1. Who am I to embarrass him?

2. I know that television time is too valuable to be taken up by quibbles about what genre I work in.

3. I have always fancied being known as a major novelist.

You can't clip little things out of television news and mail them to friends. Whereas my friend Jim Seay frequently sends me items from the *Batesville* (Mississippi) *Panolian.* There it is, for instance, in black and white: The Batesville Job Corps Center women's basketball team is known as the BJCC Warriorettes. I didn't make this up. I could show you the clipping.

Newspaper news does not show facial expressions. This means that a newspaper reporter can snarl the whole time he is writing an account of crooked shameless shenanigans among people who make more money than he does, and not have it held against him in the libel trial.

Television reporters, on the other hand, may well make more money than the crooked shameless shenaniganizers in question, and therefore they have more perspective. It shows in their faces.

On this point, by the way, could I just say one thing? Why in the name of heaven do the hosts of *PM Magazine*— or *Evening Magazine* or whatever the locally hosted, coming-up-right-after-the-network-news potpourri of extremely soft news is known as in your viewing area—*smile* so grotesquely? These people can't get through a simple sentence without beaming, simpering, and very nearly *chortling*. Are they high on something? Possessed by some neo-religious bliss? Over-influenced by commercials?

I'm sorry. I'm beginning to slip over into opinion. I want to make it clear that the following is not news but an editorial, which may or may not be concurred in by the management of this publisher. Here is the following (or, as TV anchorpersons sometimes say when a commercial is coming, "And now, this"):

The hosts of *PM Magazine* should be pelted with rolled-up copies of the *Los Angeles Times*—*wet* rolled-up copies of the *Los Angeles Times*—until they sober up.

You can't do upper-arm-flab-reduction exercises while reading a newspaper. By the same token, there is no such thing as a newspaper dinner.

YOU CAN MOVE YOUR LIPS

The first time I ever felt a girl inside her blouse was because of a book. A novel I bought in a drugstore. In it a sympathetic character of about my age felt a girl inside her blouse, something I had thought just wasn't done (or, more to the point, allowed) by a decent young person. The girl responded, literally, the same way the girl in the novel did, eagerly. So that's one thing I owe to reading.

On the other hand, recently I got to JFK's Pan Am International Terminal half an hour early, to make sure I was there when an extraordinary woman named Christabel arrived from London. I planted myself where I couldn't miss her when she emerged from customs, and as I waited I read Coleridge's *Christabel,* which is a *strange* damn poem. I got so wrapped up in it that I didn't see her go by, and it was forty-five minutes before we found each other.

But I can't help it, I love to read. I love the discretionary rhythm of it, so much more sustainable than that of eating or even drinking or even anything else: oh wait slow down mull that again go back again, never quite getting it all. The joy of text, cerebrolingual, aurilabial; the threads and knots and slippages; the weft of phoneme and notion. An intense rush may come from listening to speech, but speech, even if audiotaped, is not there in your hands to *peruse,* until it is set down in letters and becomes something else. Once I tuned in on the Joe Franklin television talk show at an inexplicable moment. I wish I had it on cassette, but it pleases me even more written down:

FIRST GUEST: Is it Da-Da [pronounced as a baby might] like Da-Da art?
FRANKLIN: Yes. I think.
SECOND GUEST: D-A-H.
FRANKLIN: D-A-H. But the *H* is silent, like in the word *fish*.

There is so much margin for error in English! And personally I would not have it otherwise. To me a little minimalism goes a long way, for this reason: Minimalism doesn't fool around enough. I want some (organic) *swash*. Robert Frost said, "I like to drag and break the intonation across the meter as waves first comb and then break stumbling on the shingle." But it doesn't even have to be that complicated. Here is a sentence I like, from *At Swim-Two-Birds:*

"It is my mission here this morning to introduce you to a wide variety of physical scourges, torments and piteous blood-sweats."

The Irish! More Flann O'Brien, from *The Third Policeman:*

"I put my hand in my pocket to see if my wallet was there. It was, smooth and warm like the hand of a good friend."

"Walking finely from the hips the two of us made our way home in the afternoon."

"We were in an entirely other field by this time and in the company of white-coloured brown-coloured cows."

I would not necessarily relish hearing any of those sentences read aloud. I love to hear people, or at any rate children (my daughter at six, to a friend: "I'll hit you so hard you won't be able to see straight except for the mean monster and the cruel thieves that beat you"), talk. But literature is what's lost aloud. Your tongue can't quite manage it, that's why there's a need for writing; but the most pleasant reading is that which your tongue can, and with relish does, *imagine* managing. (I enjoy the word *relish,* a good tonguey word.) The lines you leave most fondly behind are the ones that lead your tongue and lips and ear and palate in a dance in your mind. (Sense makes me want to say "in your head," but I yield to sound.) Kipling:

> *The temper of chums, the love of your wife, and a new piano's tune—*
> *Which of the three will you trust at the end of an Indian June?*

A newspaper headline:

STUDY SEES LAG IN LAWS
ON USE OF HUMAN TISSUES

The name of a television station in Austin, Texas:

KTBC-TV

Why is "KTBC-TV" such a pleasurable thing to say, either soundlessly or aloud? It has the rhythm of a whole, periodic sentence.

> *Kay* tee bee *See,* tee *Vee.*
> *Here* must I *stand, alone.*
> *What* an ab*surd* rou*tine.*
> *Don't* let it be the *end.*

The rhythm evokes falling downstairs—the pell-mell rush, the pause in midair toward the bottom, then, bump-bump, the coming to rest.

Then there are all the rhymes. But "Mamie E. Lee, be free!" hasn't the same charm. These call letters almost seem to have more *meaning* than that sentence. Are there subliminal echoes of "Oh say can you see"? Does KT almost seem to be a (bouncy) character? "Katie be seated please." Does TBC suggest tuberculosis and Before Christ bizarrely run together? Or am I making all this up?

"TB" and "TV" rhyme—are in fact almost the same (with echoes of "To be or not to be"?), closer in sound than "believe" and "bereave," for example.

> *Kay tee Bee,*
> *See tee Vee*

would be a couplet of sorts. But as hyphenated (semantically as well as grammatically), what we have is

> Kay *tee bee* See,
> *tee* Vee.

This keeps resisting, just barely, the reader's efforts to resolve it into a balanced metrical pattern, yet it clearly holds together in some strong way. Like a dream perception, trying and always just failing to focus on a situation that seems to be coherent and yet not.

But the key to the whole thing may be oral gymnastics. The great but negotiable clutter of all those consonants. *K:* tongue way back. *T:* way up. *B:* tongue back, lips in action. *C:* lips open, middle of tongue lingering against roof of mouth. *T:* tip of tongue up, middle down (tongue pancakes like a fish). *V:* back up front with lips, no tongue. Maybe if you watched a tongue and set of lips moving through those letters it would be athletically impressive.

Maybe "KTBC-TV" would work as a mantra. It is a tongue twister, but not: It ties the tongue in slipknots.

But it's not all mouth, the pleasure of reading. Mental images are more or less integrally involved. Room for abuse as well as haplessness in that "more or less," but it is fascinating to come upon a trope in which you can't *tell* whether sound or image is taking undue advantage of the other. Discussing the current undervaluation of Dylan Thomas, Seamus Heaney mentions "the interface between the back of the throat and the back of the mind." I love to walk—as finely from the hips as may be—in big cities, where mannalike reading abounds. In New York I passed a deli with a sign outside that said:

SOUP TO-DAY
CALM CHOWDER

The life of letters. Consider *phlegm* and *phlegmatic*—the way that hard *g* comes out, from nowhere so to speak. (Speaking of phlegm, I told my daughter once, when she was little, that I felt bad. She said, "How?" I said I just, generally, felt bad. "Oh," she said; "my bottom teeth hurt and when I lie my head down my nose-run goes into my mouth and when I sniff it back it just comes back.") It is a strange language, and yet I swear it is essentially phonetic, even onomatopoeic, because my mother taught me to "sound out the words" and to love reading. Written English dawned on me as she read me the Br'er Rabbit stories. We cannot abide it, anymore, when the author refers to the "venerable darky," but when Joel Chandler Harris and Uncle Remus get to narrating in concert, they cook. *Tooby sho. Bimeby.* Inventive oralists produced those elisions of *to be sure* and *by and by,* and the folklorist pulled them out of the air by means of spelling. I have never understood why so many readers are put off by the difficulty of written dialect. What is English, anyway? Take the word *bulb.* No one would call it dialect, nor would anyone say that it was authored. But *bulb* is a dialectic achievement. I have heard different people pronounce it "bub" and "bullub," but of course it is right in between—and so close to, yet so much more elegant than, *blub.* To pronounce *bulb* is to sketch a bulb in your mouth, with no waste motion. To spell it is to refine the process further.

Who dared first come out with *bulb?* How did that person know that other people would know what it meant—or *did* know what it meant, even when they nodded? Okay, maybe *bulb* was easy. An onion may have been the first bulb, and it may have been named in a synesthesial flash, the way people name a dog Woofy.

I don't want to get sticky, but children may come up with many words, the way they name their grandmothers. My mother was Mumu the last thirteen years of her life, compliments of my daughter. Once my son asked my daughter. "Why are there so many motorcycles around here?"

She answered, "All our friends are going for a rumpity ride."

"Rumpity?" I said too quickly.

"I didn't say that," she said. It could be that everyone begins linguistics poetically and then realizes it is not sociable to speak so directly from the interface of self and world.

Okay, *bulb*. But how about *would*? Who came up with the word *would*? Or the word *word*? How did those gristly neologists know how those words would be read?

I associate reading intimately—by no means entirely comfortably—with my mother, who couldn't breast-feed me but did infuse me with love and phonetics. She had a writerly gift herself, though she wouldn't admit it. Didn't want to deal with it. Had too many other things to deal with. (There would have been a great writer, who combined my mother's rich desperation with my bent toward publishability.) Here's something she wrote me in a letter:

> I had my first hospital duty. Of all people it was Julia Edwards. [She was a fat woman in our church.] She came in late, was hurrying down the hall. She still wears those high heels like we used to wear. She is big you know. We don't know what happened, but she fell. She hit on her seat rolled like a U down her spine and hit her head so hard it sounded like a water melon falling.

"Would you the undulation of one wave, its trick to me transfer"—Walt Whitman.

Lady Lovelace, Byron's daughter, said of Charles Babbage's Analytical Engine or Arithmometer, a protocomputer (this was back when the tongue still presumed that nothing could be fashioned that it could not describe): "The Analytical Engine weaves algebraic patterns just as the Jacquard loom weaves flowers and leaves."

The word *text* (also *architect* and *technology*) derives from the Indo-European root *teks-*, to weave. If you want to have some fun, dig down into the Indo-European–root appendix of the *American Heritage Dictionary. Threph-; wegw-; swombho-; bhergh-; regwos-; legwh-; gher-; ghengh-; ghrebh-* (to dig); *gheu-* (to pour); *aiw-* (vital force, life—whence *ever, aught, aye, nay, primeval, eternal, eon*). You can hear the language groaning to be born.

My children love reading but less obsessively than I do. That is probably just as well in many ways, for them and for their children. But what if the reading faculty atrophies in the culture? Back in 1980, I wrote something which derives from my mother's knee, but which no one would publish because it was too onerous to read. Another objection was that it sounded (presumably invidiously) black, which I doubt. Here it is, some of it:

> Ah-yaaaah *read*in' craze. That's right: check it out y'yeh the *read*in' craze.
>
> Get *back*, get *back*, with some olduhs 'n bettuhs, yehhh. . . . Abey-seedy, *a*bey-seedy, eeeyef: *lettuhs.*
>
> Hear me tell about it: little lettuhs on papuh, People: Right . . . *down* . . . there . . . in b'b'b'lack and white. *Yehhh* . . . uh, gimme that oooold software.
>
> Sexy let me showya the big trend goin'. Lexy let me showya*bop* to what it's owin'. Bompy-daaaaahm . . . boomp. *Read*in' craze.
>
> Sooooo . . . stay home, light a candle, dig out a volume. Left-a-right 'n' left-a-right, on . . . down . . . that colume. *Read*in' craze.
>
> Let's scope out some histori-ori-orical *back*ground, Muchachas. *Read*in', yeah. Goes back to Sir Herbert Read, Poppuh, the Englan-

dic philo-sopphuh. You ain't just thumbin' papuh, Jack 'n' Jenny, you swinging off into an *ancient* rite. Hmmm? *Got* to *love* it. Of old, there was a tribe, the Librarians. Who believed—get back— *read*in' transported you to faraway lands. Hey, don't look at me. Check it out. Ruh*read*in' craze.

You gonna plunge in. *Got* to, *got* to: I *knooowwwwww* you gonna plunge in. But first, let me do you this: a few tips, All Y'all, from the wooo-experts, man:

Uh-one. *Whoa!* Don't plunge too *fast*. Unh-uh, *hear* it: you can tome thy sweet self out. Brush up on y'Readin' Pro-gram three-four times, Patooties—I bet you ain't had that floppy hummin' since A&S Survey.

And uh-two. Read 'n' skim, for sure, yeah, read 'n' skim, Chickylickin'. But let's do the deal *right*, Folkses: keep repeatin', yehhhh, the *reader's mantra:* "What's Arthur *gettin'* at here, ummmm. What's Arthur *gettin'* at here, ummmm." *Arthur,* do you love it? Arthur was a god, Lovelies. Go on, *follow* him/her, he/she's dead.

And uh-three. Think lin-e-ar, Kids. Start with the Ishmael, get an easy r'rhythm goin', keep your sweet yinyang pluggin' toward they call it the Finis.

And uh-*four*. Don't dance, Brethren. You can't dance to readin', man. Talkin' *Gutenberg* reaction, physi-*depro* time. Ooo-chi-*hua-hua*.

And uh-five. Sexy just because you're *read*in', yeh, uhunh, don't mean . . . *you* know what I meannnn: Hey *aw*right, you can flash a little bicameral mmm-no*stal*gia, Sweets, but don't, like, scramble them deeeeep-set precepts, hunnnh? *You* know. Don't hog consciousness. *You* know. Don't block will-o'-the-weal. *You* know.

Well, there was more of it. About hitting the Wall of Longueur, and so on. I'll tell you this: I am glad to have typed it up for the last time.

"The written word has its limits," said the Emperor K'ang-hsi (seventeenth century) of China, "for the primal sound in the whole world is that made by the human voice, and the likeness of this human voice must be rendered in dots and strokes." But the problem is deeper than that. I was trying to get at something deep-structural in that reading-craze piece, but I failed, bottom

line, to please. A man named Philip Francis Little, according to
Oliver St. John Gogarty, wrote:

> *The aim that all we poets have in writing is of pleasing*
> *Ourselves, which is the object each one has when he is sneezing.*

Which pleases, but doesn't suffice. I won't read anything without
a contract. A contract endlessly deconstructible, to be sure (that
goes—or I wish would go—without saying), but nonetheless
phenomenal. Paul Valéry wrote: "A metaphor is *what happens*
when one *looks in a certain way,* just as a sneeze is what happens
when one looks at the sun."

You know why I cite that? Because *I* sneeze when I look at the
sun. So did my father. And I used to assume everyone did. (But
I find that most people are surprised to learn that anyone does.)
And so, evidently, when he wrote that, did Valéry.

That's the chance writers take. *Appreciative* readers are tickled by that presumption.

SITTING ON A SEESAW

(Bringing the Month's Rejected
American Poetry into Focus)
by O. V. Wiener

. . . . . .

If one were constrained, under the conditions of this sort of journalism, to sketch hastily the central purport and character of the disregarded American poetry of the past few weeks, one might well postulate a sort of teeter-totter.

On the one hand—or seat, that is—there weighs the stern concentration on, almost the heady obsession with, the lack of any purport and character at all in the world about and within these poets. As Owen Frisian concludes in some of the most resonant of the recent overlooked poetry:

> *I don't understand what principle is at work here*
> *I don't understand what principle*
> *I don't understand*

And on the other seat, not quite strong enough to cancel or even to balance permanently this first tendency, there is the pressure of a perhaps all too ready, even factitious, arrogation, often however in a very tiny way, of an ordering grip on life—a tendency also reflected by Frisian, in a second poem.

> *I've had a pit in my mouth since April—*
> *A material pit, that I*
> *Divested of an olive,*
> *And that would make a tree. It's mine.*

Frisian, in his *Mud and Other Poems* (turned down by Knopf), tends in this way to swing back and forth from poem to poem, and therefore (a pity, since he is refreshingly in command of his means for one so young) to cancel himself out.

A poet who does not cancel herself out, at least not in this way—who adheres stoutly to the affirmation seat—is Lydia P. Messenger, whose *Lines for Then and Now* has just been sent back to her, at special fourth-class rate, by Random House. The author of "To a Youthful Friend" ("The Library lions don't really care?/ Oh, come, I think they do") and "Take Heart, Executives, Blood of the City" ("Now hop a subway pulse to the heart of town/ And spurt to work") is at bottom, one feels, and primarily, a pleasant-minded woman, who does not yield to the temptations of strident feminist trumpeting—as have so many recent poetesses manqué not considered here (because they have all yielded to the temptations of publishing themselves or each other). But Messenger doesn't stand up to scrutiny, after all.

The recently ignored poet with perhaps the most total commitment to the other—the denial—end of the board is Trini Uhl, whose unprintably titled slim volume (last seen by Menemene Press), which brings together his entire output of nearly forty years, goes on mostly in this vein:

> *Oh*
> *Oh*
> *Who can even*
> *Know for sure*
> *His soul is rotten*
> *Oh.*

In his only other mood Uhl assails everyone whom even he might be expected to value.

> *Camus sold out . . . to the Leading*
> *Family Spray Come on Down Sartre!*

Au Go-Go Come
On Down Sartre! Au Go-Go Come on. . . .

There is something almost appealing about Uhl; but if his tropes occasionally charm, his attitude eventually grates, and we look for a less uniform spirit, a talent willing to grapple more widely on the board.

However, one of the boldest of recent failed poetic efforts—virtually a heroic one, at first blush—seems to be an attempt to break away entirely from this seesaw oscillation. No one is likely to come along soon who handles, or finds, language as Emory Groth does. In *Closing Glories* (just returned by University of Maryland Press) he calls to mind Stevens, Lowell, Dylan Thomas, even the later Yeats (and someone else difficult to put one's finger on—Rilke?), and holds his own, in a sense, in that company. It is hard to believe that throughout a volume of twenty-eight long poems such a pitch can be maintained as in these lines from "Homeopathic I":

Night hones no sleek charter here
In metastatic umber: Not until
Its plumaged hover grind
To siftings of Susannah
(Sheer . . . shudder . . . sheen)
Must you chirm that heavy arpeggio
Peggy o'mine.

But Groth's capacity for sustension is perhaps his downfall, for in the end so much robust diction rather wearies, and, further, when we look away from the language and rhythm to Groth's ideas, I fear we find his back turned; until he turns around, we must be persuaded that Groth breaks away from the prevailing up-and-down pattern only by failing to be truly contemporary—by failing to be in on, as we might say, the real pumping.

Thomas Flute has always been a difficult unsuccessful poet to classify, and on the evidence of *Flakes and Others* (lost last week by Munford Printing and Publishing Company), he still is. Flute seems a very nervous sensibility, and his susceptibility to abrupt transcendence must finally be met with some reservation by the more even-tempered. What is one to say, for instance, of this passage from the title poem?

> *I am issuing note after note*
> *No doubt faint but at large; they remind you*
> *Of snowflakes: not much but they float,*
> *Have their shapes as they fall; there behind you*
> *Sweet Jesus! goes God in a boat.*

There is unquestionably an immediacy here, as in many of Flute's shorter poems, that is remarkable; but one could wish it were achieved at less expense in the way of unity of tone.

A new voice, which might almost have been a truly interesting one, is heard in Grant Moon's first rejected volume, *But O! My Eyes Are Clean* (Old Directions, just folded). This sprawling stretch of verse implies some talent, but on the whole that talent is drowned in essentially arid surges perhaps typified and self-convicted by the recurrent "Oh, I'm full of it this morning." Before it can engage in any sort of significant action on our figurative board, this verse wobbles from the piquant to the banal in a single line ("Charon me back to cold Virginny, you swinging old bugger Art"), and at length dissolves—notably when Moon attempts to deal with material beyond his grasp (Logical Positivism, the sea)—into utter chaos, in which the ground for pushing up and down is completely lost and the board shakes off all riders and begins to rotate uncontrolledly into a clattering blur.

An established unpublished talent, to which we might hope to look for an effectual steadying, resolving influence, is that of Ina Tomey. Tomey has been producing poetry now, along with supportive criticism and a novel-manuscript of near permanence, for the better part of a decade; her considerable following of close friends and editorial assistants will be both rewarded and made, one suspects, increasingly impatient by her latest book. In *Bundles* ("This one's not for us either"—Valerian Press) Tomey has as usual invested considerable resources and determination in generally attractive, even at times compelling, lyrics; but, as usual as well, one finds the curious lapses from aptness that no one can ever talk her out of. The poet who can speak of "Oh,/ Those golden slippers,/ That glisten, and are gone," is also the poet who can write

> *Clouds*
> *Were substantial as mattress-batting:*
> *Near at hand;*
> *Cows*
> *Seemed almost to tiptoe*
> *In the quiet*

—the latter of which images is strained, out of nowhere, and, as anyone who has ever really attended to cattle's gait in the quiet can attest, just wrong. But try to tell her that.

Perhaps, finally, the most finished and telling of this poetry is to be found in Avram S. Mistresson's *Misgivings: 9* (personal letter from someone at Viking). His is a fine steady command of all the tools: epitomized in the nice irony, the innate tact, of the refrain (in "Song") "The behavioral sciences do not mind"; or in these lines, with their deftly calibrated, carefully modulated off-inner-rhyming and universality, from "Reflection":

> *That I be not wasted*
> *I aim to write a poem.*
> *That someone who knows*
> *Knows is a poem.*
> *How do they know?*
> *I can taste it.*

Whatever the subject of the poems here—loss at badminton, hurt animals, an unknown Puerto Rican woman and her child—Mistresson brings to it just such imagery evenly apt, rhythm and sentiment firmly balanced, a lyricism keen if sometimes fading. Such disciplined, well-earned tension is the result, we may infer, of an acceptance, a willingness to deal with the stiff pivotry of the seesaw—down around the heart of the fulcrum, as it were. And here then may stir the potential by which the going pattern might legitimately be broken, the whole teeter-totter shunted horizontally forward—if, that is, such a poet as Mistresson can ever indeed generate the requisite torque, the heft, which are sadly lacking in these poems.

SUMMERTIME AND THE READING IS HEAVY

A feeling seems to have arisen that summer is the time for light reading. I don't know where anyone got that idea. The truth about summer is this. There are an enormous number of hours in it—slow hours—and yet, before you know it, somehow it is over. So all you have to do is to start reading Heidegger, say, on the first day of summer. One day you look up and both summer and Heidegger are done.

Summer is the time for heavy reading, reading that works up a sweat. I wouldn't be surprised if there were scientific studies showing that the sun's heat melts eye glaze. People are forever leaving Proust behind in summer cottages. "I was in the process of reading Proust from cover to cover to cover to cover last summer, " people say all winter, "and then a lot of sand and coconut oil got in the part about Albertine and the dairy maid. . . . Tell me. This is something I've been wondering about. Is it your feeling that the dairy maid was actually a man, too?" But people do read *some* Proust in the summer. And next summer they find someone else's Proust in the new place they rent—a Proust in which nothing has been spilled—and they read some more.

Are people going to read Proust and make a living at the same time? No. Not ordinary people. Ordinary people are going to wait until they are at the beach, and the phone is not constantly ringing off the hook, and the only discouraging word is the sound of gulls squawking overhead. That's when they are going to read Proust. Some Proust. Things feel heavier in the summer. Whatever you pursue in the summer is going to be heavy, even if it's Ed McBain. So it might as well be Melville's *Pierre, or The Ambiguities.* Which is not Proust, but does go on and on, and does have dialogue in it like this: "Can it? Can it? No—yes—surely—can it? It cannot be! . . . What can this bode?"

The thing to do is to set the summer aside, quite firmly, for all that heavy reading you have been meaning to get around to. "This summer I'm doing the deconstructionists." No one ever says, "This spring I'm doing the deconstructionists." Because in spring you are on the lookout for the first jonquil. I don't care what T. S. Eliot said about April, it is no time for the deconstructionists.

Summer is a different matter. The jonquils are finished. Your sunburn is such that the touch of a zephyr is like steel wool. In the summer you could read the *Cantos* of Ezra Pound. There is something unreal about the summer anyway, isn't there? Summer is when you see horseshoe crabs and Portuguese men-of-war. If these things exist in a civilized society, then why not great but completely insane poems about usury?

When it's summer, people sit a lot. Or lie. Lie in the sense of recumbency. A good heavy book holds you down. It's an anchor that keeps you from getting up and having another gin and tonic. Many a person has been saved from summer alcoholism, not to mention hypertoxicity, by Dostoyevsky. Put *The Idiot* in your lap or over your face, and you know where you are going to be for the afternoon.

What better time than summer for some really dense Faulkner? It's always hot in Mississippi, isn't it? Do you think you can make sense of *Light in August* in Connecticut in February? Do you think anything is light in August in Mississippi, or in Faulkner? Why do you think people write such hefty, seething stuff in South America? For two reasons: (1) Because they have read Faulkner. (2) Because it is hot in South America.

People evidently write in a kind of molten mode when it's hot. Profundity comes boiling up. It follows that people *read* in a kind of molten mode when it's hot. Profundity gets boiled right back down. No need to burn the midnight oil in summer. Heaviness can just be soaked up. I know a man who, in his youth, caddied for so many people who kept copies of *War and Peace* in their golf bags that when he was assigned that great novel in college (summer session, fortunately) he was able to read it in eleven days, which is four under par.

Russia is another interesting case. Russia is not known for being hot. And yet its literature is known for being heavy. Perhaps the truth is that heavy literature blooms in extremes of temperature. In most parts of this country, the closest we can come to the extremity of Russia's wintry cold is by lying out in the sun in July in the middle of the day at the beach. Pinned down helplessly by Goncharov's *Oblomov.*

But you say you have read all the heavy literature produced down through the ages. First, are you sure? You've read Sartre's *Being and Nothingness*? You've read it through a couple of times and sorted it all out, as to which is which? (Being is fall, winter, spring. Nothingness is summer.)

Okay. Here are the new heavy books for this summer's reading.

Imperfect Instincts, by Franz Glodz. The gravamen (a good summer word) of this demanding work is that the only way of living authentically is by getting in touch with one's instincts, bearing in mind that one's instincts are radically wrong, and exercising certain largely doomed corrective techniques. After reading this book, you may well not feel like doing anything. What better time to feel that way than in the summer? What is there to do in the summer anyway? Play tennis? Do you really think there is anything authentic, deep down, about your backhand?

Your Parents Didn't Love You, by Ciel LaVolf. Dr. LaVolf argues persuasively that your parents, at least if you were born before 1967, never really cared anything about you, and therefore they saddled you with a resentment toward them that you will carry to your grave and pass on to any children you may ill-advisedly have. Ignore Dr. LaVolf's message at your peril.

All About Flies, by Jo Tzwilitz. Sound like a lightweight subject? Not so. What Miss Tzwilitz has done here is get flies down, once and for all. In the process she answers such immemorial, swarmy-day questions as "What do flies want from me, anyway?" She has translated the language of flies, and given us access to "fly-arias" in which flies reveal, at droning length, that what they basically want to do is to eat something—just what, is not clear—in our hair.

This Was, by Garth Pflug. The subtitle of this 486-page confessional poem with no punctuation (except for one comma, which will make you jump and weep and forevermore appreciate commas) is *Even Harder on Me Than It's Going to Be on You but Not Much.* Enough said.

Life's Adjustable of Chaos, by Vliet Von Vargueles. You thought *Finnegans Wake* drove you crazy? Did you keep thinking, while reading *Finnegans Wake,* "If I could just come upon one straight phrase, even, that just sort of sounds like a normal person communicating"? Well, this new book is even more so, and longer. So rife is this new book with quintuple semi-entendres that if you could get cable television where you are, you would throw this book away. If the bluefish were biting where you are, you would throw this book away. If any halfway decent-looking sand dollars ever washed up where you are, you would throw this book away. And yet, you find yourself not throwing this book away. Because it is literally too heavy. And it costs $27.95. (Note: According to a rather pleading letter from the author's wife that was inserted in the review copy I received, the book's title is a pun on "Life is just a bowl of cherries.")

Holy Toledo, by Lembeck Thule. This is nothing less than an imagistic survey of the complete sprawling religious spectrum of Toledo, Ohio, presented as a kind of masque—now satirical, now theological, now dialectical, and always in dialect. Not exactly one's preconception of Ohioan speech sounds ("udge" is used for "of" throughout), but rather a whole new ecstatic language. Entire sermons, exactly as preached in actual Toledan services, are rendered as they would have sounded if anyone in Toledo actually spoke this way. It's tough going, but the effects are uncanny.

Uhhhhhh . . . Uhhh, by Hideyo Imi. A thirteenth-century Japanese epic poem, translated into English for the first time, which recounts the moving of Mount Ishi to the top of Mount Oh, boulder by boulder, by sumo wrestlers. The last 3,200 lines of this opus make the schlepping scenes in *The Naked and the Dead* seem downright airy, but a sprightly opening section gets you in the mood to put your shoulder to the task:

> *Welcome, distinguished reader. I would like you*
> *To read this mammoth epic instead of haiku.*

So slip on your goggles and your reading trunks, for the sun is high.

Let me leave you with one more thought. In what season of the year do we find ourselves—I'm speaking for a moment in terms of the physical world—*wading through* things?

Surf. Kelp. Books.

Summer.

SOIL, THE SOUL
OF BALL

. . . .

In the little bitty Massachusetts village where I live, white flecks like cold dandruff are sauntering arrogantly down from on high to join the heavy white topping that has glazed over everything for months. The only visible thing resembling dirt in this entire area is the sand in the roadways, and I am feeling an intense *nostalgie de la boue*.

My son plays hockey; in youth-hockey circles there is an almost panicky appreciation of a commodity known as "ice time." Got to get out there on that ice whenever it is unoccupied, from 4 A.M. to midnight; can't waste the ice's time. How about my time? And how about *dirt* time? It is good to know that elsewhere in this favored land spring training is under way and people are dusting their hands and bat handles with dirt or rubbing dirt into new balls to cut the slickness or digging into dirt with their spikes or scooping grounders up out of dirt or hurling themselves all out through the air to slide roughly but smoothly, to schuss, through dirt.

Ah. This is a tribute to baseball's unbroken connection to earth. Baseball remains the only American sport that has not dispensed altogether, in any arena, with American soil. In sixteen of the twenty-six big-league stadia the grass is still real, and even the most thoroughly carpeted parks have patches of high-grade dirt at home plate and the mound, for pitchers and catchers and hitters to root in, and at the bases, for runners to slide in. There was, at a minor-league park in Portland, Oregon, in 1969, one game played on a completely fabricated surface, with vinyl "sliding granules" strewn at the approaches to the bases. But that experiment failed. Runners would hit those granules and keep on sliding, sliding, sliding, right on past the bases and sometimes as far as the stands. Good.

A football game, of course, is often played wholly on a rug, and consequently no dirt or grass stains appear on the players. Only smears of stickum, snot, and blood, which can't be seen from the stands. By the fourth quarter, virtually pristine gridders look unreal, like mechanics sliding greaseless from under cars.

Football lore would be far poorer if games had always been played on carpets. Big Daddy Lipscomb, though a huge, fearsome tackler, had a dread of small creeping things. Once when he was playing on sod for the Steelers he bolted violently offside for no apparent reason. In explanation he pointed a great trembling finger at the ground: After he had taken his three-point stance a worm had come crawling up out of its hole right next to his knuckle.

After the University of Tennessee's football field was covered with Tartan Turf, the UT football team had to have a dirt boy. One of its managers was designated to bring along a bucket of dirt for every home game because quarterback Bubba Wyche felt he threw better with a dry, dirty hand, and he insisted that rosin didn't help. Baseball today may need agents and stepped-up security and lawyers, but it doesn't need dirt boys yet.

I was a big fan of Dirty Al Gallagher, who played for the Giants and the Angels some years ago. "I really liked Montreal," he said once. "Montreal has some real funny dirt. You can really get filthy. The dirt is *dark* dirt." But he also liked the dirt in Anaheim Stadium, which was a mixture of red clay and brick dust that was prepared by the stadium's groundskeeper. "The great thing about the dirt here," Dirty Al Gallagher said, "is that you can't get rid of it. It comes through your uniform the next day."

One sunbaked August afternoon in Yankee Stadium, I was watching Vida Blue pitch Oakland to a competitive 5-3 win. This was before A's owner Charlie Finley took the fun out of baseball for Blue, and before the designated-hitter rule took pitchers out of the offensive game. Pitching, hitting, and running with a will on this parched day, Blue had worked up a wholehearted sweat. He had got so juicy by the eighth inning that he slid into third in a big cloud of dust and came up with his back covered with mud.

Ballplayers can't be afraid of getting a little dirt under their fingernails. And there are at least two other ways in which baseball is like farming.

One: Baseball's grass-roots popularity and local social importance, major leagues aside, have historically been greatest in rural areas, where open space and long, not to say vegetative, summer hours are most plentiful.

Two: Baseball buds in the spring, blossoms and ripens all summer, and yields its harvest in the fall.

It is worth noting that even with the disappearance of flannel, all the essential elements of baseball—ball, bat, glove, rosin bag, and player—are biodegradeable. High-speed photos show the bat bending in its arc like a sapling. The glove is kept supple by application of neat's-foot oil, which is rendered from the feet and shinbones of cattle.

Granted, synthetics have affected the nature of the game. Man-made turf, a faster surface, puts a greater premium on human speed, offensive and defensive. It also cuts down on the individuality of grounders. I remember talking to former *Sports Illustrated* writer and ex-bush-league second baseman Mark Kram about ground balls late one night in a Chinese bar. Old-fashioned treacherous grass-cutting bump-hitting organic grounders were what drove him out of professional ball, he said. He spoke gravely: "I can still see some of them coming toward me. Like certain snakes." On unnatural turf, grounders become more like rockets and less like animals.

A person can make an *impression* on dirt. Dick Allen, who said about Astroturf, "If horses won't eat it, I don't want to play on it," also once expressed himself, and drew Commissioner Bowie Kuhn's wrath, by writing COKE, BOO, WHY, NO, WHY again, and MOM in large letters in the base-path dirt with his foot as he played first base for the Phillies. Another time Campy Campaneris, then playing for Oakland, wrote a whole narrative in the dirt. It was in Seattle, in a cozy park called home by the now defunct (and even then unqualified) Pilots. Campaneris led off a day game by hitting a little squiggler down the third-base line. As several Pilots watched it squiggle, in hopes it would squiggle foul, Campaneris reached first base and headed for second.

A two-base squiggler?

No. The Pilot third baseman snatched it up just before it exhausted itself and pegged it to first. Campaneris made a frantic circle and beat the throw back.

And there the whole play lay recorded in the fresh infield dirt: the first baseman's footprints coming straight to the bag and Campaneris describing 360 degrees and ending in still-unsettled dust. Like the ripples from the day's first dive into a swimming pool—except that these prints persisted, less and less distinctly in the company of others, until the whole palimpsest was dragged smooth by the grounds crew after the top of the fourth.

Dirt. Remember how it felt as a kid when, after fantasizing about such a thing for years, you actually made a *full-length diving stab of a wicked line drive,* and you got up and shed dirt from your glove and threw the ball with a puff of dust and shook the dirt off your entire person and found your cap and banged it against your leg to get the dirt off it and maybe there was even a little dirt in your shoes you had to shake out, and you sensed all over yourself a certain richly merited patina, and the other team was yelling in *terrible barefaced unvarnished envy,* "Okay, Mr. Hot Shit, play ball!"

WHY IT'S 10:10
IN THE WATCH ADS

For when the One Great Scorer comes
To mark against your name,
He writes—not that you won or lost—
But how you played the Game.
—Grantland Rice

Winning is fun; losing is hell.
—Billy Martin

I hoped that my researches into the matter of winning would verify something I had long suspected: that the word *triumph* derives from the Roman custom of requiring the vanquished to say "umph" three times. No such luck.

I have learned, however, that the roots of the word *win* go very deep, perhaps all the way back to a Hittite verb meaning "to copulate." *Win* is a branch of one immemorial tree whose diverse other sprouts include *Venus, venerate, venison,* and *venom*.

I have also at long last figured out, to my own satisfaction, why it is that advertisements for watches—watches with hands—almost invariably show the time to be somewhere between 10:08 and 10:12.

V for victory. Rocky frozen with his arms upraised. Actually, Rocky may have stood at something closer to 11:05, but it's the same principle. People eternally tend to take sides and to want their side to win. Watchmongers know this.

So do people in the sports business. Life, history, and serious literature seldom provide examples of outright uncontestable victory, but sports does every day. In sports, what's won won't come unwon. Sportspersons who win get to keep on making a living by playing games, or by managing those who play games, or by hiring and firing those who play or manage. Sportspersons who lose, don't. One way or the other, sportspersons tend to get pretty grim. So how come we call it "playing" and how come we call them "games"?

I promise this will not be another of those "Are we placing too much emphasis on winning and thereby losing track of the true purpose of sport?" ruminations. For one thing, I'm not sure what the true purpose of sports is, aside from moving the runner on second to third with less than two outs.

On the other hand, when was the last time you read one of those ruminations? Isn't it getting a bit thick lately, all the talk about winning, being a winner, in sports and out? Thicker even than usual? And is anybody even complaining about it anymore?

"Wanna be a winner?" asks a television commercial. "Buy a Chevy." What? Are people running home to their families these days and shouting, "I won! I won! I bought us a Chevrolet!"? I wouldn't be surprised.

In this country today, 220 books are in print whose titles *begin* with the word *Winning*. Only the One Great Scorer knows how many other available titles contain some form of the word *win*. Here are just a few:

A Winner's Notebook, Be a Winner, How to Win at Office Politics, How to Unlock the Secrets of Winning & Good Luck, Win the Happiness Game, Act Like a Winner, Dressing to Win, It's Your Turn to Win at Work & at Home, Why Winners Win, Choose to Win! and *Z-Cycle: Winning by a Force of a Fourth Type*.

I don't know what a force of a fourth type is, but more and more it seems that Americans are being divided into two types. The business news is full of coups: the overtakers taking over the overtaken. A magazine ad for Puma sneakers shows George Brett of the Kansas City Royals poised to swing his bat with a vengeance, and the caption reads: "ATTACK. Because if you're not the predator, you're the prey." The Republicans—led by a man who once made a baseball movie called *The Winning Team* and a football movie in which he played the person referred to in the phrase "Win one for the Gipper"—have had a dynasty going.

The Democrats through most of the eighties have been too abject to be identified with any television program, unless it is *One Day at a Time*. The term for a social misfit in high school these days, I gather from my children, is "loser."

How can anybody in America relax and have a good time anymore, if every morning presents anew the question "Am I going to win today?" Even the defense establishment seems to feel insecure. One bright A.M. late in 1985, the *New York Times* reported, "The Reagan administration, rejecting proposals for delay or compromise, began a high-level lobbying effort today to win a showdown on the MX missile." Fearful that Congress would "kill the new missile," the administration was eager to win overwhelming congressional support for it before the Easter recess, when congressmen were seen likely, in the words of a Pentagon spokesman, to "get their brains beat out by every church group, every Mother for Peace." I didn't even know there still *were* any Mothers for Peace, and yet the military-industrial complex is afraid it can't lick them.

Can this prevailing state of mind be explained by the notion that we now live in a "zero-sum society," in which any one faction's gain is another's loss? Or is fallout from America's no-win situation in Vietnam (and now in the Middle East and Latin America) to blame? You can't win, trying to answer questions like that. I will attempt only to make a few points. About winning, its relativity, its limitations.

"Winning is the ethic of football," Don Shula, the head coach of the Miami Dolphins, once said. "You start with having to win, and you work back." It must be noted that the most insistent talk of winning in sports comes from coaches and managers. That's because a coach or manager's won-loss record is his only statistic. He must win to have coached well. But that doesn't mean Shula is out of line.

If all you care about a sports event is who wins, you can't appreciate it fully. But neither can you if you don't care at all. To get into a game wholeheartedly you have to root. And to play a

game wholeheartedly, at its highest levels, you must go all out—
not to look pretty or enjoy the way the playing surface feels
under your kangaroo-skin shoes, but to win. Falling in love is
solipsistic unless it involves winning another's heart.

But romance is not pretty if it aims to *squelch* another's heart.
The 1985 final National Basketball Association playoff series,
between the Los Angeles Lakers and the Boston Celtics, should
have been a beaut, but for me it was spoiled by Boston's con-
stant harping on intimidation. The Celtics kept implying that the
Lakers lacked character, would fold; to prove their point, the
Celtics' big men tried to beat up the Lakers. As it happened, the
Lakers called upon their own heavy bangers, Mitch Kupchak and
Kurt Rambis, who busted heads effectively enough that Los
Angeles (thanks also to magnificence from the stately Kareem
Abdul-Jabbar and the Celtics' forgetting how to make the ball go
through the basket) wore Boston down. But only one of the six
games was delightful. That was the fourth, won at the buzzer by
the Celtics. "There is so much *spunk* in this game," exclaimed
Tom Heinsohn, the telecaster, and he was right. But the kind of
courage shown in the series generally had too much to do with
pressure and not enough with grace.

Winning is the ethic of sports in the sense that, as a novelist
once said, credibility is the ethic of fiction. The integrity of
sports lies in trying to win, not to show off. Players must be
determined to win if fans are to suspend their disbelief.

But nobody wants to read a novel whose narrator keeps
crying out, "By God, this story is credible! No, dammit, now it's
losing credibility! I'll see about that! These characters *better* be
credible, or I'll kill them off!" That is, in effect, what George
Steinbrenner—the most visible owner, unfortunately, in
sports—keeps saying about his Yankees. When they lose, he
apologizes for them publicly (though he is constitutionally un-
apologetic about himself). He accuses various Yankees of having
"spit the bit." He takes it upon himself to assert that Dave

Winfield, whom he acquired for the Yankees and who is one of baseball's best players, is "not a proven winner." He dismisses managers obsessively. He does not understand the game.

"Winning isn't everything," said the late Vince Lombardi, revered head coach of the Green Bay Packers, "it's the only thing." You have to give Lombardi credit. He produced great teams, and his players, at least in retrospect, said they loved him. The kind of drive he apotheosized is America's motor. If life were based on need, rather than hustle, then whining might be regarded as everything. The athlete's will to win is one of those primal amoral urges—like the businessman's to maximize profits and the journalist's to get the word out—that our system takes as a given. And competition is not an exclusively capitalistic tool. It was Marx who said: "The proletarians have nothing to lose but their chains. They have a world to win."

It is worth reminding ourselves, however, that Lombardi's famous saying is crazy. The only thing that is everything is everything itself, and not even sports can be boiled down any further than to the binary W/L. If winning were the only thing it would not be such a big deal. And we would not treasure the memory of Joe Don Looney, Bo Belinsky, Johnny Blood. There wouldn't even *be* any Chicago Cubs.

When I heard that Angelo Dundee, the trainer of Muhammad Ali and Sugar Ray Leonard, had a book out entitled *I Only Talk Winning*, I was at first dismayed. Dundee is widely regarded as a decent, affable, hardly monomaniacal man. I felt better when I read the book's last paragraph:

"I've called this book *I Only Talk Winning* for a reason. In life, there are positive and negative thoughts. And hey, it doesn't cost you a cent more to think positively. *I Only Talk Winning* stands for 'Don't be afraid of losing.' Losing is nothing. There is no such thing as failure, only learning how."

Literally, I guess, that, too, is crazy. It comes off a bit over-rosy compared with, say, these lines by William Blake:

They win who never near the goal;
They run who halt on wounded feet;
Art hath its martyrs like the soul,
Its victors in defeat.

But, hey, could Blake handle fighters? I like what Dundee says, because it rises above venom, aversion, compulsion.

Something else I like is a memory from the 1973 NFL play-offs. I had spent that season hanging around with the Pittsburgh Steelers to write a book. The Steelers had just been trounced by Oakland. Their campaign had been a failure, in pro football terms, because it had not ended in ultimate victory. I had stood with the players on the sidelines as Raider fans threw things at us, reviled us, cried out in the nastiest of tones, "You guys are *lewsers.*" The following season the Steelers would win the first of four Super Bowls, and I would celebrate that triumph, which was sweet, on the sidelines. But this was a losing locker room. And yet here's what Andy Russell, the Pittsburgh co-captain, told me, his eyes shining:

"I was into that game. There was no other world outside it. There was nothing. That's the thrill."

"Does that make it hard to lose?" I asked.

"No, easier. You know you gave it all you had. Some games you're distracted, by an injury or something, and you get down on yourself, question your character. This game I was away, into the *game*. We lost. But all I could think afterwards was, 'Damn, I had fun.' "

Another thing that 10:10 on a watchface looks likes is a smile. Smiling time. Playtime. Recess.

Remember recess? I in fact don't, very clearly. Ballplaying, threats, bullyragging, all a blur. But it must have been fun. I vividly remember fidgeting in my desk longing for the clock to come around to recess time, sweet surcease from improvement. I craved to get away from intellectual activities, which at the time I was embarrassingly good at, out there onto that rough tumbling ground, even though I felt capable of whipping only one or two boys who counted, and I didn't have any real desire to whip anybody.

Once I thought I did. This kid named Gerry Worley sat in front of me and I was eager to dissociate myself from him because he talked like a grown-up, in measured, unidiomatic terms, and he wore *slacks* (probably his father's, cut down) instead of Levi's and shiny brown shoes instead of sneakers, and everybody hated him.

I let it drop that I couldn't stand sitting behind him any longer and I wanted to beat him up. This attracted attention because I had never beaten up anybody. An occasion was arranged at recess, some of the other boys and I following Gerry around until he asked what the matter was. That was just like him: He didn't get blustery or blubbery, he acted *concerned*.

"Roy's gon' beat you up," one of the boys who actually fought a lot said.

And Gerry, who I suddenly realized was pretty good-sized, said the most mature thing I had heard a contemporary of mine—even him—say:

"I don't have any quarrel with Roy."

I just sort of huffed around, realizing he was right, and worked my way into the background, where I have remained, a reporter.

I also remember, in the third grade, looking out the classroom window at Scooty Petrie walking around on the playground slumped over. During recess he had lost some little thing, a knife or something, that his father had given him. He was the only kid in our class whose parents were divorced, and his father had just visited him.

Not even the teachers liked Scooty Petrie. He was the only kid you wouldn't want to play with even if your parents didn't want you to play with him. And they didn't—when Scooty was about nine he and his younger brother actually shot flaming arrows onto some people down the street's roof.

But Mrs. Loftus, our teacher, who never seemed to have a soft spot for anybody, certainly not Scooty Petrie, had let him stay out there and search. She was looking at him when I went over near her to sharpen a pencil. She said so quietly that only I could hear her, "He's out there crying his little heart out." He was walking all around; it was a big scrabbly playground.

And then he bent down, jumped up, and it was like a movie scene—Scooty Petrie all by himself through the window out there jumping. Found it.

A hush fell over the room. Because people had been talking louder and louder among themselves and Mrs. Loftus had turned, become herself again, and hollered, *"Huush!"*

But that's a postrecess memory. Nothing recedes like recess.

Scooty Petrie—not his real name—is now an arbitrageur. No, I just made that up. But I do remember standing by that window and realizing that anybody could feel sorry for anybody, without sacrificing professionalism of course, and it might do some good.

Roy Blount, Jr., is the author of eight books that have gotten progressively shorter until this one, which is just about the right size. He is from the South, lives in the North, regards the eighties as a trashy decade, and has two children who have gotten progressively longer. As former president of the senior class of Decatur (Georgia) High School, he cannot foresee any circumstances that would cause him to resume an active role in politics—more active, that is, than going *"Plpp!"* when public officials are mentioned. He weighs about one hundred and eighty-five pounds.